The Darkness of Globalism

The Darkness of Globalism

Exposing the Vicious, Violent, Murdering Ideology

COLTON WESTON

ISBN-13: 9781548080686
ISBN-10: 1548080683
Library of Congress Control Number: 2017910468
CreateSpace Independent Publishing Platform
North Charleston, South Carolina

This book is dedicated to my hardworking Mother, Wanda,
And to all Working-Class People Across Pennsylvania
And Across America.

Table of Contents

Preface

Thankful

I want to start by saying that there's a lot to be grateful for in our Country right now. So let me first start by Thanking God for the Victory of President Donald J Trump. Thank God for the Courage, Endurance, Conviction, Cunning, Intelligence, Stamina, Wisdom, and Leadership of Donald J Trump and his toughness to stand up for our Country. Thank God for Vice President Mike Pence and his personal strength and common sense. Thank God for an Incredible Victory for 'We the People' and for the spirit of freedom, common sense, and prosperity. Thank God for a chance and a real opportunity to save the Greatest Nation in the History of the world and all of the Western Civilization along with it. Thank God for the liberty and freedom we have in America. Thank God for the freedom to write this book. Thank God for our founding fathers and for the Constitution they gave us. Thank God for George Washington and Thomas Jefferson. Thank God for the Continental Army and the Americans that fought against the British Crown in the Revolutionary War. Thank God for all those who fought, bled, and died for America and its ideals. Thank

God for the US Military service men and women who protect us. Thank God for the Police that upholds the law. Thank God for the working class people and middle class across America that works hard every day and is the backbone of this Nation. Thank God for Single Moms who work a million jobs doing everything they can to provide for their children. Thank God for those who are brave enough to speak out against a rigged economy, a rigged media, a rigged political system, and a rigged biased educational system. Thank God for Authors like President Donald Trump, Roger Stone, Wayne Root, Milo Yiannopoulos, Ann Coulter, Dinesh D'Souza, Laura Ingraham, and many others. Thank God for Trump supporters in Pennsylvania and across the rust belt and the country. Thank God for the ability and freedom to go to a Donald Trump rally in support of the 1st amendment. Thank God for Real Media like Infowars, Breitbart News, and Drudge Report. Thank God for positive people who want America to succeed and the middle class to succeed. Thank God for Good Teachers who love America. Thank God for terrific people on YouTube like Paul Joseph Watson, Stefan Molyneux, Mark Dice, Bill Whittle, and others who stand up for common sense in a variety of ways. Thank God for people who don't want to send America and the world back to the third century. Thank God for people who volunteer at homeless shelters, soup kitchens, clothe drives, salvation army, and the American Red Cross. Thank God for people who give blood to American Red Cross. Thank God for farmers who produce our food. Thank God for Tea Party conservatives who don't want the IRS to be able to politically target opponents. Thank God Hillary Clinton lost. Thank God President Trump doesn't owe anything to special interest groups. Thank God we get to 'Drain the Swamp!' in Washington. Thank God we get to 'Make America Great Again!'. Thank God America is blessed with an abundance of Natural Resources. Thank God President Trump takes the threats of terrorism seriously and isn't afraid to name the enemy. Thank God President Trump understands the value, security, and importance of having a secure border. Thank God President Trump knows how to rebuild our Nation's crumbling infrastructure. Thank God President Donald Trump understands the importance of renegotiating failed trade deals. Thank God President Trump is cutting taxes, especially on the middle class. Thank God people who make under 25,000$ a year will get tax relief. Thank God we have a President who takes National Security and National Defense seriously. Thank God we have leadership that will cut the out of control federal red tape and the stifling regulations hurting the economy. Thank God we're abandoning Obamacare and government-run health care nightmares in favor of free market solutions which will lower the cost of care and increase the overall quality. Thank God we have a President who understands how to create jobs "Big League" and create quality middle-class jobs. Thank God we can now start taking the National Debt seriously. Thank God we have somebody who understands 'The Art of the Deal' and can negotiate successfully with the Communist Chinese Government. Thank God we have a President who knows how flawed, rigged, and biased the educational system is against conservatives on Ivy League campuses. Thank God we have someone who takes cyber security seriously and will defend our intellectual property rights from being stolen by the Communist Chinese. Thank God we can start taking care of our Veterans properly and give them the care that they deserve and they earned by serving our Country. Thank God we can now have a legal and sane immigration policy that puts Americans and America first. Thank God Hillary Lost by an electoral landslide. Thank God we don't have Bill Clinton back in the white house. Thank God we have a person who is a world-class businessman and understands how to get things done. Thank God we have a Vice President who was a successful Governor and knows how to create jobs and the importance of following the constitution. Thank God President Trump has assembled an incredible Cabinet around him of highly successful people who know how to get results. Thank God there are still good people left in America and in the world. Thank God for my Lord and Savior Jesus Christ. Thank God Jesus died for our sins. Thank God there are people who value the American Flag and everything it represents. Thank God America can now come back bigger, better, stronger, and more exceptional than ever before!

One

Introduction

The reason for writing this book is very simple. To give voice to the millions of Americans who have been hurt by Globalism in one form or another. I'm not a conspiracy theorist, and I don't deal in conspiracy theories. This book is about addressing FACTS. Whether it's because of horrible trade deals, insane immigration policies, corruption, crime, lack of opportunities, the debt, biased liberal universities, living in the highest taxed nation on Earth, crumbling infrastructure, radical Islamic terrorists killing innocent people, or the corrupt lying media engaging in censorship, the threats from globalism are seemingly limitless. So much tragedy has happened to our country as a result of letting powerful international elite run rough shot over us and have unlimited control over our nation's economy, politics, media, culture/entertainment industry, energy, domestic policy, foreign policy, immigration policy, and just about everything else. The average working people, working class, middle-class person who just wants to climb the rungs of the social and economic ladder has been hit so incredibly hard and from so many different directions simultaneously that it's challenging for them to even know where to begin.

Let's talk about students, for example. What about students who don't want to go in a socialist direction? What about students who don't want free things from the government? What about students who want free market solutions to our Country's problems? What about students who believe in the rule of law and common sense? What about students who supported President Donald J Trump for President? Well what happens, of course, is that they are labeled a racist, a bigot, a homophobe, a xenophobe, a Russian agent, 'Islamaphobic,' a bully, a hater, and a dangerous individual. They are censored, ignored, given unfair treatment, lied about, smeared, demonized, and worse. They are given a student loan bill for a degree they earned by attending a college or university that fundamentally disagrees with everything that they believe in. They are sometimes viciously physically attacked for going to a Trump rally or just because they support Trump in general. They are graded more harshly than other students who don't wish to question registered Democrat "Professors." They are marginalized and made to feel unimportant.

What about small business owners in America? The job creators of America. How are they treated by a globalist influenced government establishment? Well for one, they are taxed into oblivion, bankruptcy, and anywhere in between. Tremendous amounts of money they worked for and earned through hard work, creativity, and ingenuity is stolen from them and is given to Authoritarian Government slave masters who despise the fact that they would dare to try and survive without government assistance. They are forced to attempt to understand a complex 90,000 page U.S. tax code that nuclear physicists and some of the smartest people in the world can't even comprehend or begin to understand. They are told by Obama that when it comes to their business, that they didn't build it. That's right folks, let's remember the 2012 election quote from then President Barack Obama running for reelection at that time: "If you were successful, somebody along the line gave you some help. There was a great teacher somewhere in your life. Somebody helped to create this unbelievable American system that we have that allowed you to thrive. Somebody invested in roads and bridges. If you've got a business, you didn't build that. Somebody else made that happen."[1] So there you have it. You didn't grow your business. Now, it is true that there are great and incredible teachers out there. It's true that the founding fathers sacrificed a lot to create this country. It's true that so many Brave heroes sacrificed everything and gave their lives to defend America and its principles. It's true that because of America's free market system and other freedoms from the Constitution, that we became the most powerful nation ever (which is why so many other countries and globalists want to bring us down, is because they simply can't compete with us when we are trending in the direction of more free market, more freedom, and more of the American dream). It's true that every successful person has had at least some help along the way, or else they wouldn't be human. But to suggest that when it comes to your own business, whatever that happens to be, that you didn't build it. Well, that's just nuts. But then again, so is Obama.

Additionally, another thing that happened as recently as December 2016 is worth pointing out. As millions of Americans were getting ready for Christmas, going to see a new Star Wars movie, shopping, drinking, eating Christmas cookies, wrapping presents, etc. Obama very sneakily and very quietly, with as little attention as possible, signed into law the 2017 National Defense Authorization Act (NDAA) which gives hundreds of billions of dollars of funding to the military.[2] So what is so significant about this, you ask? Well, included in this 2017 NDAA, hidden very deep and away from the public, who have little interest in such things and are much more concerned about the NFL, is the "Countering Disinformation and Propaganda Act".[3] Now, when I read this it terrified me to the core, and you should be concerned as well if you're living on planet earth. Apparently, this also includes the creation of a "Global Engagement Center" and when they say "Engage" that doesn't mean that they want to be your friend.[4] It means they want to silence you. Let me be as direct as possible. This law allows the government to collect, store, and search through records of *ANYONE* that is considered to be spreading propaganda or disinformation. This includes all of us. This includes Americans citizens. This is dangerous beyond words. This is insanity. This is a government gone mad. This is tyranny. Senator Chris Murphy (D-Connecticut) said that "This bill is primarily dedicated to countering propaganda and disinformation outside the United States" which is a lie. The original version of the bill included a provision that explicitly stated that anti-propaganda or anti-disinformation efforts by the "Global Engagement Center" will only be done with the effect to influence foreign audiences. That provision, however, was removed from the final version, which was just signed into law. What does that mean? This means you. This means you should be concerned. This means that even if you're born in the USA like I was born in Pennsylvania, you could be labeled. Even if you've never been outside the USA before, but the authoritarians in our government deem you to be some kind of disinformation agent, you could be labeled. What if the authoritarians that are still left in our government don't like this book? Well, I guess this all just leads down a slippery slope of censorship. A slippery slope that eventually leads right off a cliff. This "Countering Disinformation and Propaganda Act" is something that hurts my soul. I don't want censorship for anyone. I believe in free speech. Even if there are leftists or Democrats or anyone in America with a different opinion than me, I don't want to censor people. They should speak out and write books of their own. Just don't censor me or any other American. Plus, who gets to determine what is considered to be disinformation and what is not? Who gets to decide what is "fake news" and what is not? Who gets to determine who has free speech and who does not?

Another important reason for the writing of this book is to give voice to people in the Tea Party who were unfairly targeted not just by the rigged, corrupt corporate media; But were also targeted by the IRS for the crime of simply having a political opinion. How evil of them for daring to have a political opinion. I think it's important to always remember what happened to the Tea Party and conservative groups who were viciously targeted and attacked illegally. The failed so-called "mainstream media" has entirely abandoned even mentioning this huge story years ago. CNN, ABC, NBC, CBS, MSNC, CNBC, New York Times, Washington Post, etc. simply don't care. They didn't care when the Obama government and the IRS and other agencies targeted these groups. Even the IRS itself has since come out, over three years later, and admitted that it was over 400 different conservative and tea party groups that were targeted in this enormous scandal. Flashback to 2013, the IRS was then claiming at the time that the number of conservative groups which were targeted was under 300 (still an insane number) and we now know that that was a lie by the IRS's own admission. Who remembers Lois Lerner pleading the 5th over and over and refusing to testify? I'm really sick of the IRS and all their garbage.

I also want to mention all the Trump supporters who have been so viciously assaulted and physically attacked. We cannot go numb to this kind of senseless violence, cowardice, hate, chaos, and insanity. I think it's important to stand up to these radical, third world mentality criminals who chose to attack Trump supporters. A good man and Trump supporter named David Wilcox was brutally beaten by a group of attackers.[5] Captured on video, you can hear the words yelled "You Voted Trump?! Damn, he voted Trump" as he is outnumbered, assaulted, and even dragged behind a car. Another incident caught on video, which also happened in Obama's incredibly dangerous warzone-hometown of Chicago, shows an incredibly brave and courageous young man being kidnapped and tortured in an evil hate crime. The details of this video are so horrifying. Nobody should have to go through what this hero went through. These hateful, evil, torturers have been charged with kidnapping and hate crimes. Then you've got A 74-year-old man who was assaulted and thrown to the ground by a 23-year-old female Black Lives Matter activist outside of Trump Tower during a protest. The attack occurred after he shouted "All Lives Matter." The assailant, an "anti-bullying activist," was arrested. In Stafford, Virginia an elementary school student was horrifically beaten by his own "classmates" for voting Trump in a mock election and was taken to the Emergency room. A high-school student in the Sunshine State punched another student who was holding a Pro-Trump sign. The person was arrested and charged with felony battery. When he was taken to the dean's office, he reportedly started tearing the room apart and said, "When I see that white boy again, I'm going to punch him in his face." There are countless more examples of violence, including thugs literally getting an entire Trump rally canceled in, yet again, Chicago, one of the most dangerous places in the world. Let's never stop talking about this violence. Let's never give in to violence. Let's never stop condemning those who make calls for violence. Let's not be bullied by thugs. Let's not be intimidated by trash who hate America.

Sadly, this type of violence is just the tip of the iceberg. Let's discuss the impact that terrorism has on Western Civilization. Because of the incredibly dangerous, globalist, failed, corrupt, weak, and evil "leaders" we've had in Europe and the United States we've had an influx of Islamic terrorists into the Western world which is truly horrifying beyond words. An overflowing stream of people coming from some of the most barbaric parts of the world who don't even understand the concept of civilization itself. People who only believe in Sharia law and are totally incapable of wanting to understand our Constitution, obey our Constitution, assimilate constructively, or even be peaceful at all. Despite what multicultural extremists say, the fact is that all cultures are not equal. An Islamic culture where women are treated like animals is not equal to ours. Where women must wear a veil, must be accompanied by a male when they leave the house. An Islamic culture that beheads people regularly. A primitive culture which commits genocide against Christians, Gays, and Jews. A culture that is still in the third or fourth century and never found any type of renaissance, enlightenment, or transcended in any real way. The so-called "Islamic State" is nothing more than a group of incredibly dumb violent animals that hate America and Europe. Videos emerging last year of ISIS filth lowering people in cages into vats of nitric acid, having people beheaded, and burying them up to their head in the sand. This type of pure scum, pure evil, and sheer wickedness has to be called out and eradicated. These ISIS fighters are nothing more than propagandized tools that are being used to destabilize entire regions around the world in an attempt to destroy civilization. They won't. They will lose, and they will lose badly.

Some of these attacks on humanity include one as recently as December 2016, when an animal driving a tractor-trailer truck drove over scores and scores of innocent people walking around at a Christmas Market in Berlin, Germany. Another truck attack in Nice, France. A car used as a projectile and a mass stabbing at Ohio State University. New York and New Jersey bombings. A horrific Orlando nightclub massacre. The deadly, murderous strike on our consulate in Benghazi, Libya. The mass shooting in San Bernardino. An attack against our military in Chattanooga, Tennessee. ISIS militants publically executing at least 52 people in Mosul, Iraq after Iraqi troops entered the city. Car bombings in Turkey. A suicide bombing attack against our American Airforce base in Bagram, Afghanistan. Countless Suicide bombings in Bagdad, Iraq. A suicide bombing attack in Yemen killing at least 50 people. More car bombings in Istanbul, Turkey killing at least 48 people. More civilians publically executed by ISIS trash in Iraq. Soldiers burned to death outside Aleppo. More car bombings in Syria. Another mass shooting in Libya by the Islamic state. Another attack here domestically, a Fort Lauderdale airport mass shooting. There are thousands of other attacks against humanity and lets of course never forget what took place on September 11th, 2001. Let's take a moment and pray for all these victims of terrorism here in the United States and around the world. Let's also pray for their families. Again, I'm thankful we now have President Trump who takes these threats seriously, and we can now begin to successfully name, identify, and defeat these enemies of humanity. President Trump understands that we can never Make America Great Again until we first Make America Safe Again.

An additional reason for writing this book which is very important to me is to give thanks to our wonderful police officers and military veterans. Our incredible veterans are some of the most amazing people in the world. They are incredibly brave and have served our Country with courage, honor, and strength. It's totally unacceptable to me to see what has happened to the Veterans Administration and see the corruption, incompetence, and bureaucracy get in the way of taking care of our heroes. The fact that so many veterans commit suicide each day is absolutely heartbreaking and unacceptable to me. Veterans who are broke and homeless and are living in hell on the street. We cannot let this continue. We absolutely need to start giving the best health care in the world to these people, and it needs to be done in a way that is responsive, effective, efficient, and actually puts the veterans themselves first. It's such an insult to see these brave warriors fight for our country and the freedoms we value, only to come home and be treated like dirt and have to wait in line, forever, only to get third world quality health care. Their health care should be nothing but the very highest quality and they shouldn't have to wait and they shouldn't have to pay a dime. We should also start valuing our veterans more in society in general. This means saying thank you to them. This means following the constitution they fought for. This means honoring them, appreciating their courage, and thanking them for their service to America. We also need to start treating our terrific police officers much better. Whether they are local or state police, the fact is that these people put their lives at jeopardy every day to protect us and uphold the rule of law. It's very unfair for the police that all we hear from the disgusting failed television networks is negative news about the police which makes them look like monsters and jeopardizes their safety and increases tensions between civilians and police. The fact is, the police are the only thing we have standing between chaos, insanity, and evil. They protect us from evil doers, and we need our police officers of America. Let's start treating the police with the respect that they deserve.

It's now time to discuss the American worker. We are going to start acknowledging the blue collar workers of America in a big way. They are the backbone and power of our entire economy. Their hard work, even while being demonized by certain people in our country, is what makes up the fabric of America. They deal with a lot on a regular basis. They pay all the taxes. They fund the government. They deal with physical pain from the work they do. They work very hard for what little money they make and are overtaxed on top of it. They've seen horrible trade deals like NAFTA ship jobs to other countries. They've watched the roads they travel to work on deteriorating into rubble. They've watched as our bridges, highways, and tunnels have broken down over time and have become structurally deficient. They've seen their factories be shut down. They saw their jobs go to people who are in our country illegally and cannot speak any English. They've watched our nation's trillions of national debt climb and climb and climb. They watched Obozocare increase their health care premiums through the roof. They've watched their electric and energy costs go up astronomically. They've looked at a lying, corrupt, corporate media tell them how wonderful the Obama economy was when they knew it was horrible. We are going to start putting these workers first and their middle-class families first.

Finally, this book is for anyone who dreams big. Anyone who wants to attain the American dream. Anyone who intends to beat the odds and overcome their circumstances to try and make it in this country. Anyone who knows what's like to have only a few dollars in your bank account. Anyone who knows what it's like to have Christmas without the presents part. Anyone who knows how excruciating it is to watch your family struggle with bills. Anyone who wants to work hard and become successful.

I understand these challenges all too well, and life certainly throws lots of obstacles at you, and you fail and make mistakes and learn from them and grow. Growing up in Pennsylvania, I've seen our factories be shut down. I saw the economy become a total nightmare under Clinton, Bush, and Obama. I've watched our country become more and more divided. I've seen our nation become less and less safe. I've seen our debt go up like a rocket ship. I've watched a corrupt political system. I've watched a dishonest media try to take down people they disagree with. I've watched the American Dream become more and more difficult for people to achieve. I've watched people struggle. But I've also watched America take on incredible challenges that seemed impossible to overcome. As we continue with this book and delve into the different facets of Globalism, and why it's been so hurtful to America, let's keep in mind all of these people. Let's keep in mind the person who dreams of creating a better life for themselves. Let's remember the person who dreams big.

Two

Nationalism vs Globalism

What we are watching in the world right now is a Colossal battle between Nationalism and Globalism. The rise of more populist driven ideas and parties in Europe and the United States. The Brexit in the UK, the Italian referendum, the election of President Donald J Trump, and populist parties in France, Austria, Netherlands, and Germany are all positive for Nationalism in general. The idea that countries should decide their own destinies. They should control of their own culture and control their own fates. The idea that nations should govern their own citizens and make their own laws. The idea that there should be more freedom and not less. The idea that national sovereignty not only matters, but that it is what makes a country...a country. What makes it unique, special, and independent from other countries and the world as a whole. Why its history matters. Why its geographical landscape, food, music, art, fashion, literature, architecture, entertainment, and sports matter. Why its Soul Matters.

On the other side, you have the opponent, Globalism. A conglomerate of international mega-banks, billionaires, multi-national corporations, the International Monetary Fund (IMF), the United Nations (UN), the World Trade Organization (WTO), and people like George Soros (we'll get to him in the next chapter) who believe in a borderless world. To be clear, I'm not advocating isolationism for America. The United States is entirely intertwined with the global economy. We buy, sell, and trade with other countries. We absolutely need amazing diplomacy, better trade, efficient travel between countries, more safety, cooperation, and humanitarian efforts to help starving third world populations. The threat is not from us being a part of the world. The threat is from globalism and us giving up our sovereignty.

Globalism, to me, are elites who think of countries as just geographical locations with populations that need to be managed economically, educationally, politically, culturally, legally, and socially. These populations are thought of as nothing more than cattle or livestock which needs to be controlled. A controlled population is more profitable for them. It's more cost-effective for mega-banks and select corporations. It's beneficial for getting globalist agendas through. It's good for getting puppet politicians like Obama to push through whatever insane legislation he wants and leave President Trump with a mess to clean up. It's beneficial to them to have an entirely corporate mainstream media which they own and can steer in any direction they wish. Globalism is war, death, destruction, poverty, chaos, and violence. Globalism is authoritarianism. Globalism is insanity.

So how do these opposites get along? They don't. They can't. You can't get along with people that want to take away your ability to direct your own country. This is why we see this nationalism and populism in Europe and the United States. People want to be in charge of their own countries again. It's really not complicated.

Let's first discuss the incredible and historic event that was the Brexit. An incredible moment. An event that changed the world.

The people of the United Kingdom electing to leave the dictatorial European Union. Former British Prime Minister David Cameron resigning. Overcoming the European media, critics, politicians, and incredible overall odds. So how did all this happen? Let's start with the debate that went on in the UK, continues to go on, and the lead up to the Brexit vote itself. On one-half of the debate, you had the European Union, the media, the UN, European elites, mega-banks, Universities, and millions of people screaming "racism." On the other side you had brave British citizens, led by Nigel Farage, who only wanted freedom, Independence, and to walk down a path that isn't authoritarianism. Many people in the UK felt like the European Union was trampling all over them. This is because the European Union is a dictatorship controlled by unelected, unaccountable, ir-responsible, and disconnected bureaucrats that live in their own little world in Brussels.

There are many reasons why the European Union has been a com-plete and total disaster and why it has been horrible. The European Union is a dictatorial entity that covers a massive amount of the conti-nent of Europe. The EU is a classic example of how government grows and grows and grows until it's out of control. After World War II, Europe began to rebuild itself and eventually started establishing enti-ties in the 50's such as the European Economic Community (EEC) and the European Atomic Energy Community. There were also at-tempts at creating a 'European Defense Community' and 'European Political Community.' Revealed WikiLeaks documents showed us in 2009 that there was also support for a single European currency (Euro) at the 1955 Bilderberg Group. Over the decades these groups grew and expanded and eventually led to the signing of the Maastricht Treaty on February 7, 1992, which established the European Union and became active in 1993.[1] The 1994 'European Elections' had a result in which the Socialist group maintained the status as the largest party in the Parliament. After that, the Economic and Monetary Union of the European Union expanded and established a European Monetary Institute. The 1990's also included further expansion of the Euro, as currency and the European Central Bank was created. There were major conflicts in the Balkans which allowed the creation of the European Union's Common Foreign and Security Policy (CFSP). Despite this, there was the Srebrenica massacre in July 1995. The Srebrenica massacre, also known as the Srebrenica genocide was the death of more than 8,000 Bosniaks.

The European Union continued to grow and expand in power in the 2000's. In 2004 there was a massive enlargement of the EU. More countries such as the Czech Republic, Cyprus, Estonia, Hungary, Latvia, Lithuania, Malta, Poland, Slovakia, and Slovenia joined. Many European countries started adopting more EU laws in areas such as social policy, employment policy, transport policy, green energy policies, agricultural policy, intellectual property laws, science/research, financial controls, external relations, and Enterprise/Industrial systems just to name a few. Romania and Bulgaria entered into the Union in 2007 and Slovenia adopted the Euro. The European Union was even awarded a ceremonial pat on the back when it received the 2012 Nobel Peace Prize.[2] As the European Union grew in size, scope, scale, funding, and power so did the inevitable problems that come along with such unchecked power. An insufficient separation in powers and massive corruption grows. The EU constitution itself is hundreds of pages long, confusing, has insufficient checks and balances, and attempts to regulate all facets of a person's life. The EU capital, located in Brussels, Belgium, is entrenched with all kinds of special interests and powerful lobbyists. Unelected bureaucrats set and implement policy agendas with little regard for the consequences and with little regard for the peasants below them. In 2007, the former German President Roman Herzog warned that democracy was under a real threat from the EU. Between the years 1999 and 2004, an astounding 84 percent of the legal directives in Germany came directly from Brussels. Herzog said: "EU policies suffer to an alarming degree from a lack of democracy and a de facto suspension of the separation of powers."[3] This warning was brushed aside and was given very little attention at the time. The EU has systematically weakened and reduced Europe's civilization. Immigrants are considered this special protected class of people who are just being used to usher in more globalism, chaos, and government. Europe was at the center of some of the most incredible and historic achievements in all of human history. The Renaissance began in Florence.[4] It spanned from the 14th century to the 17th century. The Renaissance was an amazing cultural movement that bridged the middle ages and the very early modern age. It helped uplift, not just Europe but all of humanity through a sort of 'rebirth' and Enlightenment.[5] It included significant achievements in literature, art, philosophy, music, science, religion and other areas. Some of these accomplishments include the invention of the printing press, which was invented by Johannes Gutenberg in 1440 and allowed for Bibles, printed music, books, and other text to be to print in larger quantities. There were incredible paintings such as 'The Creation of Adam' by Michelangelo; 'The Sistine Madonna', and 'The School of Athens' by Raphael; 'Mona Lisa', 'Annunciation', and 'The Last Supper' by Leonardo da Vinci; 'Primavera' by Sandro Botticelli and many others.[6] Incredible advances in science and the scientific processes themselves occurred. Nicolaus Copernicus was a mathematician and astronomer who formulated a position that it was the Sun, and not the Earth, at the center of the Universe. He published a book called '*De revolutionibus orbium coelestium*' in 1543 which was a significant event in the history of science. There was a massive expansion of quality Universities along with new discoveries in medicine and knowledge of the human body. The idea of authoritarians and opponents of humanity throwing away this European culture and the history of mankind in favor of a 5ᵗʰ-century Islamic barbarism is absolutely insane, unacceptable, and must be called out repeatedly.

Not only is the European Union bringing in dangerous migrants and terrorists, but it also prosecutes those who would dare criticize Islam. A plethora of European Governments have made it extremely clear to their citizen-slaves that criticizing so-called 'migrants,' 'migrant' policies or Islam itself is criminality which can lead to an arrest, prosecution, and major convictions. The lack of free speech in the EU is a tremendous problem and is very dangerous. The European Union is attempting to change history and is rewriting textbooks in schools across the continent to display a more favorable image of Islam and its evil history. Under the EU's tyranny, the educational system and the media are nothing more than another arm of government. A British writer and conservative, Daniel Hannan summed it up like this by saying "Eurocrats instinctively dislike spontaneous activity. To them, 'unregulated' is almost synonymous with 'illegal'. The bureaucratic mindset demands uniformity, licensing, order. Eurocrats are especially upset because many bloggers, being of an anarchic disposition, are anti-Brussels. In the French, Dutch and Irish referendums, the MSM [mainstream media] were uniformly pro-treaty, whereas internet activity was overwhelmingly skeptical."

Newton's third law of motion states that for every action, there is an equal and opposite reaction. As this European Union tyranny has grown larger and stronger, the opposite reaction of that was citizens in the UK waking up to the fact that they don't have any say, power, or influence over their own country. This culminated in the Brexit vote, over whether or not the UK should remain in the European Union or leave. On June 23, 2016, that vote was cast and in a historic upset, "Leave" won with 51.9% of the vote (17,410,742 votes) and "Remain" lost with 48.1% of the vote (16,141,241 votes). Hats off to the British people. Good for the British people for getting their own British Independence day, June 23. I salute them for retaking their country. I salute them for standing for freedom and against tyranny.

The potential and opportunities for the British people are now incredible. They get the ability to now decide who comes into their country and have a safer immigration policy. But it's not just immigration. EU member states must allow all EU citizens to come into their country and work with no limitations. The British people now have the opportunity and freedom to control who enters their own country. They also now regain their money from the European Union and the citizens won't have to pay EU taxes. They also get to set their own tax rates. Britain was the second largest contributor to the EU (Germany is the largest). Of course, they now get to make their own laws again domestically which puts the power back into their own hands. A Pro-Leave group, 'Business For Britain', estimated that at one point 65 percent of new British laws were being made in Brussels, out of the direction of the EU. Between the years of 1993 and 2014, a total of 231 official acts of Parliament were passed because of EU membership status, a statistic straight from The House of Commons Library. One such policy is the EU's common fisheries policy which attempts to control and share EU fish stocks and gives fishermen quotas for what they can catch. This forces up prices for consumers, forces the dumping of millions of dead fish back into the ocean, and hurts fishing fleets. Britain can now grow and expand its economy independent from the EU, which means that they can buy what they want and from where they want. They can gain a competitive edge by looking for more efficient producers in a wide array of industries. This includes, but not limited to, steel, concrete, meat, grain, butter, and millions of other products. This competition will lower prices, and they will be able to do more with less. This will reduce inflation dramatically and will benefit the poorest people by giving them cheaper grocery bills, more choice, and more economic opportunities. Britain's trade deals can now be improved because negotiating will be a lot easier. It's simpler to deal with other countries and make trade agreements when you don't need consultation, advice, and consensus from dozens of other nations who are members of the European Union. What Britain does with this new found freedom is up to them. That is what freedom is about. It's is about making choices. They can make smart and dumb decisions in regards to economics, politics, media, banking, regulation reform, and everything else. The key thing is that those decisions should now be theirs to make for themselves.

When it comes to the battle of Nationalism versus Globalism, the Brexit was just the beginning. A new Italian referendum also happened in December 2016 which was very significant. Italian voters got the chance to decide on a proposed constitutional law. The bill was put forth by then Prime Minister Matteo Renzi and his party. By an astounding margin, the proposal was rejected. The "No" vote won with a massive 19,419,507 votes (59.1%) and "Yes" lost with only 13,432,208 votes (40.9%). Italian Prime Minister Renzi then resigned following the results. This result was widely seen as another huge victory for populism and the third major win worldwide in just a few months. There was also great excitement, and incredible voter turnout as more than 65% of eligible Italian voters turned out and cast their ballot.

There is also currently a rise in populism in many other countries such as France, Austria, Iceland, Germany, and the Netherlands to name a few. Terrorism, crime, economic malaise, instability, high taxes, dishonest and corrupt media, poverty, bloated bureaucracy, and tyranny, in general, stemming directly from Globalism have resulted in citizens from various countries all over the western world standing up to reclaim their freedom and national sovereignty.

But nothing was more amazing to me than what happened right here in our own country, the United States of America. History was made when we elected the 45th President Donald J Trump in a monumental victory. Trump took on the entire world and won. The pundits on TV could not have been more wrong. Sean Hannity explained this by saying "To me this was predictable, but on the other hand this is a modern-day political miracle you're witnessing before your eyes right now. And that is to go up against everybody — all the pundits and all the pollsters and all the prognosticators out there and defy all the odds. It's the American people who have said, 'Enough is enough!' They're tired of the corruption. 'The cesspool.' 'Draining the swamp.' All of these things are resonating."[7] This victory was personal to me because I was a Trump supporter from the very start. I remember watching Trump at CPAC before announcing his candidacy. I remember him talking about basic common sense things, such as how wasting trillions of dollars in the middle east is a waste of time, money, energy, and human lives. I remember him talking about how our Airports, like LaGuardia Airport, are literally falling apart and how it is a third world airport. I remember listening to him discuss how China has a stranglehold on the rare-earth minerals around the world, such as Lithium in Afghanistan, and is stealing our wealth. When he announced he was running for President in 2015 It wasn't a difficult decision for me, I knew he was my man right away. I listened to the idiots on the television networks laugh at him. I listened to them call him names. I listened to them say he would never become the Republican nominee. I listened to them say how poorly he would do in the primaries. They were all wrong. President Trump and the American people took on the entire world and won. We took on the media, the whole political establishment both democrat and republican, the globalist establishment, foreign countries, political agitators, special interests, and the politicians all while being outspent, and still, we won. I watched him defeat what seems like a million Republican primary challengers, some of whom like John Kasich and Jeb Bush did not even keep their word when they pledged to support the eventual nominee. I watched Trump and my fellow supporters get attacked in so many different ways. I watched people go to rallies, and I saw the enthusiasm there first hand. I saw the energy, passion, and patriotism of thousands of individuals at a Trump rally in Pennsylvania, it was unbelievable. I saw 'Make America Great Again' hats, t-shirts, buttons, yard signs, and bumper stickers everywhere. I saw something so incredible on November 8th that left me speechless. I saw my home state of Pennsylvania vote Republican for the first time in a very long time. I saw the entire rust belt of Wisconsin, Michigan, etc. vote for Trump. That so-called Blue Wall never had a chance in hell. I saw President Trump win in an electoral landslide. We defeated Crooked Hillary. We restored our country to 'we the people.' We beat the establishment. We defeated the Globalists like George Soros and his money. We beat Obama. I believe in miracles, and I believe in the American people. I believe in myself. I believe in President Donald J Trump. It's time to actually start winning again. It's time to challenge the lies of Globalism. It's time to Make America Greater than ever before!

Three

Soros

Martin Luther King, Jr. said "He who passively accepts evil is as much involved in it as he who helps to perpetrate it. He who accepts evil without protesting against it is really cooperating with it."[1] Albert Einstein said something similar "The world is a dangerous place to live; not because of the people who are evil, but because of the people who don't do anything about it."[2] Sir Winston Churchill said, "Courage is what it takes to stand up and speak, it's also what it takes to sit down and listen."[3] Churchill also said "If you have an important point to make, don't try to be subtle or clever. Use a pile driver. Hit the point once. Then come back and hit it again. Then hit it a third time-a tremendous whack."

I think it's important to stand up to sick, wicked, and evil people and to not be intimidated by them. The reason for writing this chapter is to point out who George Soros is. George Soros is a mega-billionaire globalist who funds radical leftist organizations, Democrat party politicians, and other radical groups. But this isn't it. He's also much more than just that. For far too long this guy has flown under the radar and has never been properly called out. Let's discuss who this individual really is and what he actually believes in.

Let's start with his childhood. Many already know the story, but sadly, many do not. George Schwartz was born to a Jewish family on August 12, 1930, in Budapest, Hungary. The 1940's brought the second World War. It was a time of violence, horror, suffering, chaos, and bloodshed around the world. It was also a dangerous and dark time for Jewish people in Europe who were being targeted by the Nazis. Jews got viciously tortured, killed, and send to evil death camps. George's father, a lawyer, changed the family's last name to 'Soros' so that it wouldn't sound Jewish. He bought his children fake Identity papers and they posed as Christians. George was placed in the care of a man who was responsible for confiscating the property of Jews, and he assisted this man in his tasks. By collaborating with the Nazis, George survived the Holocaust and the war. In his autobiography, called '*Soros on Soros*' he literally explains how he helped to cart away the stolen items of Hungarian Jewish men, women, and children when he was a teenager. This was after they were rounded up and transported to death camps. He claims it never even bothered him at all, and still doesn't bother him today. Soros has no personal regrets or remorse about his actions at that time. He turned on his fellow Jews to save himself. George Soros even explained this in an interview.[4]

George Soros interview in 1998 on "60 Minutes" with Steve Kroft:

Kroft: "You're a Hungarian Jew ..."
Soros: "Mm-hmm."
Kroft: "... who escaped the Holocaust ..."
Soros: "Mm-hmm."

Kroft: "... by posing as a Christian."

Soros: "Right."

Kroft: "And you watched lots of people get shipped off to the death camps."

Soros: "Right. I was 14 years old. And I would say that that's when my character was made."

Kroft: "In what way?"

Soros: "That one should think ahead. One should understand that -- and anticipate events and when, when one is threatened. It was a tremendous threat of evil. I mean, it was a -- a very personal threat of evil."

Kroft: My understanding is that you went out with this protector of yours who swore that you were his adopted godson.

Soros: Yes. Yes.

Kroft: Went out, in fact, and helped in the confiscation of property from the Jews.

Soros: Yes. That's right. Yes.

Kroft: "I mean, that's -- that sounds like an experience that would send lots of people to the psychiatric couch for many, many years. Was it difficult?"

Soros: "Not, not at all. Not at all. Maybe as a child you don't ... you don't see the connection. But it was -- it created no -- no problem at all."

Kroft: "No feeling of guilt?"

Soros: "No."

Kroft: "For example, that, 'I'm Jewish, and here I am, watching these people go. I could just as easily be these, I should be there.' None of that?"

Soros: "Well, of course, ... I could be on the other side or I could be the one from whom the thing is being taken away. But there was no sense that I shouldn't be there, because that was -- well, actually, in a funny way, it's just like in the markets -- that is I weren't there -- of course, I wasn't doing it, but somebody else would - would -- would be taking it away anyhow. And it was the -- whether I was there or not, I was only a spectator, the property was being taken away. So the -- I had no role in taking away that property. So I had no sense of guilt."

Soros has also spoken about his childhood by saying that "I fancied myself as some kind of god…If truth be known, I carried some rather potent messianic fantasies with me from childhood, which I felt I had to control, otherwise they might get me in trouble."[5] He literally saw himself as some type of messianic figure. This is the same man. The same leftist globalist billionaire financier who funds racial division and destabilization in America. Remember this the next time President Trump gets called Hitler by one of Soros's paid professional agitators. Remember this when conservatives are called Nazis. Remember this when Soros gives money to groups that riot, like what happened in Berkeley.[6]

In 1947, after the war ended, Soros went to England. It was there where he began his studies as a student at the London School of Economics.[7] He studied Economics and Philosophy. After that, he moved to New York City in 1956 where he worked as a trader and specialized in European stocks. Soros once said "I went to England in 1947 and then to the United States in 1956. But I never quite became an American." Over the years, Soros acquired more experience and wealth. In 1970, he founded the Soros Fund Management. Today, Soros Fund Management LLC has approximately 250 traders and manages tens of billions of dollars.

The acquisition of this money, power, and influence didn't come without significant controversy, however. In 1988, George Soros was interested in buying shares in French companies. The socialist party in France had lost a majority of seats in the Assembly in 86, ' and there was a new government. Jacques Chirac started pushing for a new and more aggressive privatization program. Many people, including Soros, thought that shares in these newly privatized French companies were substantially undervalued. Soros proceeded ahead with his strategy of buying shares in French companies. In 1989 the Commission des Operations de Bourse (COB), which is the French stock exchange regulatory authority, directed an investigation of Soros's transactions with Societe Generale, a leading French Bank, and whether or not those transactions should be considered insider trading. They concluded that their statutes, regulations, and case law which deal with insider trading, did not sufficiently establish that a crime happened. They determined that no charges should be brought against Soros. A few years later, however, a Paris-based prosecutor reopened the case, disregarding the COB's initial findings. This prosecutor reopened the case against Soros and some other French businessmen. The end result was a conviction of George Soros in 2005 for insider trading by the Court of Appeals. The French Supreme Court later confirmed this conviction on June 14, 2006. Soros claimed that there was no wrongdoing of any kind and that the takeover was public knowledge. He then appealed on the fact that there was a fourteen-year delay in the case going to trial. The court agreed to hear the appeal, on the basis of Article 7 of the European Convention on Human Rights. In October 2011, the court then rejected his appeal in a 4-3 decision, in which they said that Soros had been well aware of the risks of breaking insider trading laws.

In Britain, September 16, 1992, is known as 'Black Wednesday.' It is called this because speculators like Soros made tremendous amounts of money by betting against the British pound. The Bank of England wanted to vigorously buy the pound to encourage confidence and stop speculators, like Soros, from obliterating it.[8] Soros made a cool Billion dollars by short-selling the pound sterling, earning him the title "The Man Who Broke the Bank of England." What happened was that the British Government had to pull out of the European Exchange Rate Mechanism (ERM). The ERM and the pound sterling was devalued by 20%. The British Government realized that it was losing billions trying to save its currency artificially. Soros's bet paid off, and he gained a reputation as the primary currency speculator in the world. Soros is quoted as once saying "I was a human being before I became a Businessman."

George Soros also helped fund the very controversial Halliburton. Halliburton has been involved in many controversies over the years. This includes the 2003 Iraq War and the company's ties to Vice President Dick Cheney. There were allegations of corruption in Nigeria against the company, which were eventually dropped after a settlement of hundreds of millions of dollars was reached with the Nigerian government. There was a Deepwater Horizon explosion in 2010. A report released by BP indicated that the irresponsible practices of Halliburton contributed to the disaster. Investigations conducted by the National Commission on the BP Deepwater Horizon Oil Spill and Offshore Drilling concluded that the concrete that Halliburton used was an unstable mixture and caused hydrocarbons to leak into the well, causing the huge explosion. Halliburton also pleaded guilty to destroying evidence. There have been other environmental issues around the world, which includes a Halliburton facility in Farmington, New Mexico in 2006 creating a toxic cloud which forced people to have to evacuate their homes. This was the same year that Soros bought shares in Halliburton. A ForeignPolicy.com writer, Mike Boyer, reported on SEC documents which revealed Soros Fund Management LLC bought almost 2 million shares of Halliburton stock in 2006.[9] He wrote:

"Normally, I'm willing to overlook the hypocrisy of the liberal elite. If Al Gore and his Hollywood cronies want to fly around on gas-guzzling, atmosphere-polluting private jets while railing against global climate change, I'm willing to overlook it.

But the latest move by globe-trotting, hyper-liberal billionaire George Soros borders on being too much.... Soros, of course, is the dean of Democratic money giving. And Halliburton, of course, is the company that embodies everything the Democrats see as evil. Dick Cheney is its former chief, for goodness' sake."

George Soros has worked hard at creating an international public appearance of that of a philanthropist. In the early 1990's he started the "Open Society Institute," which is now known as Open Society Foundations (OSF). This helps him have a more favorable public image around the world and makes uneducated people think his only goal is to just support civil society groups around the world, advancing justice, public health, education, and human rights. This is pretty hypocritical considering what he told the New York Times in 1994. Soros told the Times "I am sort of a deus ex machina," "I am something unnatural. I'm very comfortable with my public persona because it is one I have created for myself. It represents what I like to be as distinct from what I really am. You know, in my personal capacity I'm not actually a selfless philanthropic person. I'm very much self-centered." In the book '*Soros on Soros*' he wrote "I do not accept the rules imposed by others…And in periods of regime change, the normal rules don't apply." In his mind, he is able to do whatever he pleases. He gets to determine when the "normal rules" matter and when they don't. I find this scary considering his wealth and the influence he's had around the world for decades.

In reality, he supports a radical agenda and pours billions into it, which promotes extremism, violence, globalism, destabilization, and fundamental divide and conquer. He promotes the idea that America is institutionally an oppressive nation. America isn't perfect, and we certainly have things we need to fix in our country, including foreign policy, but he doesn't want to fix America, he wants to destroy it. He's said that: "Destroying America will be the culmination of my life's work"[10] and "The main obstacle to a stable and just world order is the United States."[11] He wrote that the United States of America is a "threat to the world" and that we have become a "supremacist" nation, in his book entitled "The Bubble of American Supremacy".[12] He promotes open borders and mass illegal immigration; which President Trump will soon end. He supports the massive expansion of social welfare benefits and amnesty for illegal aliens. He is against the death penalty. He supports racial and ethnic preferences in business and academia to stir things up racially and divide people on race. He recommends bringing American foreign policy under the control of the United Nations. He promotes a bloated, failed, expensive, ineffective socialized medicine idea. He supports radical gun control efforts to leave Americans unarmed. He encourages leaving Americans defenseless. He promotes and pays professional protestors to cause problems and incite violence. He bankrolls the efforts to recruit, finance, and train leftist activist leaders. He supports out of control government and bureaucracy. He supports out of control regulations and insanely high levels of taxation. He promotes a highly radical environmentalism plan, which is not about actually helping the environment, it's about destroying the American economy.

Soros compares our friend, Israel, to the Nazis. He supports radical Islam being injected into the west in an attempt to destroy western civilization itself.

He gives money to the fascist "Media Matters" so that they can shut down all free speech in America and they can attack all the people I look up to.[13] A group which promotes Google, Facebook, YouTube, etc. censoring conservatives.[14] Media matters should also be investigated for tax fraud.[15] He supports radical groups like MoveOn.org and Center for American Progress. He is just too threatened by

America's existence. He promotes and calls for a "global system of political decision-making." Soros supports every evil there is.

Soros gave massive amounts of money to help fund the Obama campaign. He helped craft the direction of the Obama stimulus. Soros gave "advice" to Obama about how he should allocate money in the so-called "Obama stimulus plan." Soros then makes investments in the same areas where this money is being sent to. It's really basic. It's called corruption, folks. Soros met with various officials on multiple occasions in 2009 and then proceeded to go on a stock buying frenzy. He bought massive amounts of stock in Cisco Systems, Ameren, American Electric Power, Extreme Networks, Hologic, NRG Energy, BioFuel Energy, Constellation Energy Group, Cognizant Technology Solutions, and many others. They just miraculously happened to be the same companies which were getting injected with hundreds of billions of US taxpayer dollars.

Of course in the 2016 election, Soros was a megabucks donor to Hillary Clinton. It was the Clinton campaign team's mission to please the VIP Billionaire and 'Make Soros Happy.' So disgusting. There were many WikiLeaks which showed references to "Soros" in emails of John Podesta. The same John Podesta whose password was…the word 'password.' What a loser. It was also exposed by Wikileaks that Soros issued directives on crucial foreign policy matters to Hillary Clinton when she was Sec. of State. Of course, 'Crooked' Puppet Hillary followed these orders to the letter. Soros lost a lot of money by wrongly betting on Hillary, and I'm pleased about that. Soros also lost money after the election. Soros immediately got bearish on the markets after President Trump won, which caused him to lose over a billion dollars when Trump confidence rallied the markets and Soros bet wrong again.[16] He promotes people bringing lawsuits against President Trump.[17] He calls Trump a dictator.[18] He still has connections with Obama through various leftist organizations that want to disrupt President Trump's Agenda.[19] Soros is also trying to infiltrate the Trump administration through a mole, named Fiona Hill. Fiona Hill has been on the payroll of the Open Society Institute and the Soros Payroll directly.

Some people would be afraid to write a chapter about a powerful billionaire like George Soros, but in my own personal opinion, I think it would be terrifying to not write it. As we work to 'Make America Great Again' let's not be afraid to stand up to the sick, evil, globalists like Soros.

Four

Dangerous Foundations

The world's elite have a long history of setting up philanthropic foundations to "help" people around the world. But what kinds of activity do these foundations really have a history of doing? What types of scientific research have they funded? What are their real motives? What are their true goals? What have they done?

In this chapter, we will inspect a few foundations that have been set up by the elites. Some of these include the Rockefeller Foundation and the Carnegie Endowment. Some of these anti-American foundations have extensive histories of researching, financing, and implementing human population management plans which they explain in their own reports.[1] They also push social justice agendas, extreme energy policies, and direct public opinion in the ways they desire.

Let's start with The Rockefeller Foundation. Founded on May 14, 1913, by oil tycoon, and owner of Standard Oil, John D. Rockefeller. John D. Rockefeller died in 1937, at the age of 97, and the foundation was carried on by his ever since. Every year these major foundations generally release an annual report. On page 34, of the 1964 annual report for The Rockefeller Foundation, which is publicly accessible;

there is a heading which says "PROBLEMS OF POPULATION" in all capital letters.[2] The following is an excerpt from this 1964 Rockefeller Foundation annual report starting on page 34:

"PROBLEMS OF POPULATION

THERE is general agreement that the rate of population increase in many countries is menacingly high. The existence of this consensus is perhaps the most notable feature on the population scene today; such widespread awareness did not exist even twenty years ago and only in the past decade have the first national programs of population control come into being. This change in attitude has partly been forced by sheer pressure of numbers, but it is equally the result of the efforts of the growing numbers of scientists, planners, and administrators who have now received special training in the field of population studies and who today are making this field their special responsibility.

Advanced training and research in population problems are longstanding interests of The Rockefeller Foundation and are now included in one of its five major program areas. In 1964 the Foundation was able to give substantial aid in three of the four areas which, broadly speaking, make up the field. These are: demography, or the gathering of the facts and figures which help define what the problems actually are; the provision of family planning services; and public education in the subject. The fourth area, research into the biology of reproduction, has been a Foundation interest for more than thirty years and investigations in this area now attract support from a variety of public and private sources.

For the leaders of underdeveloped countries, confronted simultaneously by the massive stresses of economic and social change, the problems of population growth sometimes appear insurmountable. One reaction is to hope that in the long run these problems will solve themselves. This is not necessarily an evasion: since it is historically true that the birth rates in developed countries have declined, roughly in step with their industrialization, it could be argued that a similar decline would accompany the economic growth of the underdeveloped countries, (The argument would, however, avoid considering the different time-scale which is now in effect, since the underdeveloped countries have rates of population increase far higher than those found in the European countries during their comparable growth periods.)

Unfortunately, there is no reason to believe that Europe's history will necessarily be repeated in Latin America, Africa, Asia, and the Far East. No fully satisfactory theory has yet been produced to support all the facts of the European experience, and no principle has yet been formulated to link alteration in the birth rate to economic and social processes. It may be that the decline in the European birth rate was the result of an interplay of factors so complex as to be virtually incapable of spontaneous recurrence, and it is certainly true that anomalies in the histories of European countries have made suspect any broad generalities. For example, there is evidence that birth rates began to decline in the 8th century in France, by the middle of the eighth century in Sweden, and by about 1880 in England and Wales, Belgium, Austria, Norway, and Hungary. By the 1890 the decline was under way in Italy, Spain, Czechoslovakia, and Poland, It had begun before World War I in Russia. Many of these countries were at different levels of development when their birth rates began to fall: the onset of the decline was nearly simultaneous in Hungary and England, yet England was perhaps the most highly industrialized country of the time, and in Hungary, industrialization had barely begun. The population of England was about 80 per cent urban in 1880 and in Hungary only about 20 per cent,

It is therefore apparent that the nation as an entity is too heterogeneous to serve as a unit for the analysis of birth rate changes. Smaller, more homogeneous units are needed, and a promising start to the isolation of such units has been made by the Office of Population Research at Princeton University. A preliminary exploration by the office has shown that usable estimates can be made by province, rather than by country, and that data exist which will allow the construction of provincial estimates throughout most of Europe. The importance of these provincial calculations lies in the fact that it now seems that changes in birth rate can be much more localized than had been thought earlier. As one example, preliminary work at Princeton has shown that in the early years of this century the birth rate in the Russian province which included St, Petersburg had fallen to approximately 30 births per 1,000 population — comparable to contemporary rates in parts of Western Europe — while in the province containing Moscow the birth rate was still at the level characteristic of an underdeveloped country. The office now plans, with Foundation aid, to make estimates of birth rates in Europe at various census periods from 1850 through 1960, for about 500 population groups at the subnational level. With these more finely focused and homogeneous data, a search will then be made for relationships between change in birth rate and such variables as the educational attainment of men and women of parental age; the proportion of the population that is urban; occupation; religion; and national origin or language. The hope is to illumine the combination of circumstances in which the birth rate begins to fall."

The Carnegie Endowment for International Peace is a global think tank. The Carnegie Endowment has been pushing for carbon taxes and is pushing for a 'smart tax' for the oil sector. Deborah Gordon, the director of the Carnegie's Energy and Climate Program, wrote an Op-Ed in December 2016, entitled "What the World Needs Now Is Climate-Conscious Cohorts."[3] She wrote:

"It's not likely the United States will continue to be a reliable champion for addressing climate change in the coming years. President-elect Donald Trump's actions thus far do not bode well, particularly his appointment of Scott Pruitt, a principal architect to dismantle federal climate mitigation policies, to the helm of the Environmental Protection Agency. As it stands, a generation of federally funded climate science intelligence and public policy advancement is at serious risk.

It's was no surprise, then, when Vice President Joe Biden recently urged Canadian Prime Minister Justin Trudeau and German Chancellor Angela Merkel to "step up to the world stage and lead in facing challenges." Biden nailed it: The world needs Canada and Germany now more than ever, and climate change is perhaps the foremost challenge. It's a threat so serious and widespread that it requires solid partnerships, thoughtful leaders, clear rules of the road, and real innovation.

But Trudeau and Merkel can't do it alone. They'll need California's help too.

With an economy that rivals many other nations, California functions as a laboratory of democracy and has been a climate leader for decades. Together, this international triumvirate of climate cohorts can collaborate to change the world energy order and safeguard the global climate. Any policies they develop and any innovations they engender are more likely to be transformational if these governments act together rather than in isolation.

The most important step to address climate change is to put a smart price on carbon. Without a monetary value placed on total greenhouse gas (GHG) emissions, the market will not be able to act efficiently or resiliently. A smart tax that accounts for all emissions through the long and involved energy supply chain through producers, generators, transporters, refiners, and end users must be comprehensive and consistent so as not to distort markets. The broader based the tax, the less steep it needs to be for maximum effectiveness."

I have a better idea. How about President Trump and we, the American people get to set our own energy policies in our own Country.

Five

Propaganda Media

They've been called many things and have many names. They've been called the corporate media. The collaborator press. The traitor media. The establishment press. The globalist media. These are the people creating division in our country. These are the people who pretended to be neutral and are totally biased against conservatives. These are the people who collaborate with the Hillary Clinton campaign. These are the people who rig the Presidential debates. These are the individuals who push a radical, leftist, socialist, communist, globalist, establishment agenda. They have a trust level in the single digits. These are the people who cry on election night when Hillary loses. These are the people who love to attack and take down anyone they disagree with. These are the people who love to destroy conservatives. These are the people who love to attack, smear, demonize, and slander patriots. These are the people who use political correctness as a tool to shut down free speech in America. They don't report on the murders and crimes of illegal aliens. They refuse to talk about the trillions of debt that Obama created. These are the people who love to demonize the Tea Party. These are the people who lie about voter fraud. These are the people who support crony capitalism and the bailouts. These are the people who do everything in their power to belittle their competition like Breitbart, Drudge Report, Infowars, and The Daily Caller. These are the people who call others Fake News when they are the Fake News. These are the people who call everyone a racist when they are the ones who promote tribalism and racism. These are the people who push for destructive, Anti-American, globalist trade deals which hurt our workers. These are the people who vilify Trump supporters. These are the people who would never show the crowd size at Trump rallies and would use camera tricks to make the crowd look small. These are the people who dined at top Clinton staffers' homes days before Hillary's campaign launch. These are the people who downplayed Hillary's crimes at the state department. These are the people who downplayed the IRS's targeting of conservative groups. These are the people who downplayed the threat of Radical Islamic terrorism. These are the people who refused to talk about and actively worked to help cover up discussion of Bill Clinton's sexual assaults. These are the people who helped to hide Obama's past. These are individuals who tried to make it look like the Obama economy was fantastic when it was an absolute nightmare. These are the people who lied about Obamacare coverage and premiums. These are the people who lied about the real unemployment numbers. These are the people who said that President Trump was never a successful business-man. These are the people who said Trump wouldn't run. These are the people who said Trump would never get the nomination. These are the people who said he wouldn't win Pennsylvania, Wisconsin, Michigan, Ohio, North Carolina, and Florida. These are the people who said he wouldn't get enough electoral votes to win. These are the people who tried to smear him with dishonest and false sexual assault accusers. These are the people who continuously try to delegitimize his election and his administration. They are the corporate, establishment, globalist, leftist, dishonest, corrupt, rigged, biased, fake news, propaganda media.

We're going to shine a very glaring light on the corporate propaganda media. We will examine their endless lies. We'll discuss the divisions which they've helped to exacerbate. We'll talk about the violence they've helped to create. We'll examine how they've hurt our country's reputation. We'll talk about how they've damaged our democracy. We'll discuss who owns and controls these mercenary propaganda arms. Finally, we'll address why it's important to call out these propagandists and point out what a bunch of Anti-American, corrupt frauds they really are.

Let's begin with The American Broadcasting Company, ABC. I think it's sad that it's called the "American" broadcasting company. There isn't anything American about it. I think the 'Chinese-style Propaganda' broadcasting company would be a better name. ABC is owned by The Walt Disney Company and is part of Disney Media Networks. Before we can understand ABC, we have to first understand Disney. Disney is an enormous multinational mass media/entertainment conglomerate. The company's divisions and subsidiaries are located all over the globe. It has very diverse holdings and has resorts in Tokyo, Paris, Hong Kong, and Shanghai to list a few. There is also Radio Disney, Pixar Animation Studios, Marvel Entertainment, The Muppets Studio, Lucasfilm, Disney Consumer Products, Disney Vacation Club, and Disney Cruise Line. Disney Media Networks is one of the main branches of the company which owns and manages its various television stations. This includes ESPN (Disney owns 80% of it), A&E Networks (50%), and of course the American Broadcasting Network. The Live Well Network is also part of this group. Disney is very globalist in not just its business endeavors but also its messaging. This is evident by just watching ESPN, which I haven't for many years. ESPN should be about sports and athletics, but it has turned into something unwatchable. It's just more leftist globalist messaging, almost like MSNBC or something. People who should be talking about sports are talking about social justice warrior issues. It's very elitist and very left politically. It's extremely politically correct. The bias against conservatives is obvious. Just look at what happened to Curt Schilling. A man who pitched in the major leagues over a span of two decades, is a three-time World Series Champion, two-time National League strikeout leader, two-time MLB wins leader, World Series MVP (2001), six-time MLB All-Star, a Roberto Clemente Award Winner (2001). A man with 3,116 career strikeouts. He was an ESPN analyst with an incredible career, but still got fired for not being politically correct enough. It doesn't matter who you are, or what you've accomplished, if you don't tow the globalist, socialist, politically correct line, you get fired. Curt Schilling is a conservative and has thought about running against Senator Elizabeth Warren in 2018. I hope he does and I hope he beats her because it would be a great thing for America. The point is clear, however, that when it comes to Disney, it's all about its political correctness, globalism, leftist ideology, and big government. This is what drives ABC's coverage as well. It's what drives their narrative and talking points. It's what drives their hostility to President Trump. It's the lies that ABC news spews all the time and they are well documented.[1]

Recently, the stock market has been hitting all-time highs. The market has gained over three trillion dollars in new wealth just since President Trump was elected. The Dow Jones Industrial Average (DJIA) has surpassed 20,000 for the first time and is currently sitting at about 21,454. I realize that this wealth has not gone to the middle class or the working class who are struggling just to survive, and we've got a lot of work to do with our economy that is still growing too slowly. This wealth, from increases in the stock market, has gone to the richest people in the country. It's gone to the elites, like Silicon Valley, many of whom helped fund Hillary over Trump in the election. I understand the economy shouldn't be based off just the stock market, but if this were Obama or Hillary who got the stock market to all-time highs and added trillions in new wealth, it would be getting round-the-clock coverage from the mainstream media and from ABC. Since it's President Trump who got the stock market to all-time highs, it gets no coverage.

Aside from just being biased, networks like ABC love to divide Americans. They like to separate people. They love to get people thinking in terms of race, religion, gender, ethnicity, educational status, income, social status, and of course political affiliation. It's a basic strategy: divide and conquer. The more Americans are fighting amongst themselves on every issue, the easier we are to control and manage. Aren't you tired of the constant divisions? The continuous narrative of Black people vs White people, Rich people vs Poor people, College educated vs not college educated, liberal vs conservative, male vs female, and America vs the World. One tool ABC uses in its arsenal of division is its show 'The View.' Look at the way they treated Kellyanne Conway, the Trump campaign manager and the first woman ever to successfully run a Presidential campaign. She made history and had an incredible accomplishment. Yet, she was interrupted, treated rudely, not given proper respect, and belittled. If she were a campaign manager for the left, it would have been much better treatment.

The Columbia Broadcasting System, CBS, is the property of the CBS Corporation. CBS's coverage of the 2016 Presidential election was pitiful and full of lies. Let's start with the rigging of the polls (which is something all the media was guilty of). Propaganda Media like CBS continually pushing skewed polls that showed Hillary in a more favorable light. They oversampled Democrats on a margin that is staggering. Their efforts failed, and the American people ignored the rigged polls. Their efforts to smear Trump as a racist failed. Their efforts to ignore and demonize WikiLeaks revelations failed. In fact, it was revealed through WikiLeaks that most of the propagandists in the media took their directives and orders directly from the Clinton campaign. They were even taught how to sell Hillary Clinton to the public and how to effectively market the Clinton campaign messaging in a way that put Hillary in a more favorable light. It got so bad and so outrageously biased to the point of utter insanity.

For example, on one Thursday evening in mid-October just weeks before the election, the alphabet networks had their evening fake-news programs cover false allegations of sexual assault against Trump. They brought on women with their false allegations and it was on the networks for more than 23 minutes combined. WikiLeaks revelations revealed the Clinton campaign's blatant media collusion, their disdain for Catholics, their advocacy for open borders, and a whole lot more; that got a whopping 1 minute of coverage. The ratio of negative coverage for Donald J Trump as opposed to Hillary Clinton was literally 23:1. But it still failed. Their efforts to run with a narrative that Trump supports a "Muslim Ban" failed. The President made very clear that it's about suspending immigration from regions of the world linked to terrorism, a practical and common sense solution. Their efforts to delegitimize the Trump administration with allegations of Russian Hacking failed. Their efforts to say that President Trump is mentally ill or unqualified failed. Everything they do fails because people understand how dishonest they are.

Sharyl Attkisson is an Emmy-Award winning investigative correspondent, formerly with CBS, who talked to World Net Daily about the media's failures. She told WND that "We tend to surround ourselves by like-minded people who codify one another's misconceptions," and that "We bury our noses in the propaganda and rhetoric of political parties and corporations, adopting their narratives, instead of picking up our heads and observing what's really going on around us. I will say that I'm not a political expert, but the reason I long said Trump would win had to do with recognizing and ignoring the narratives being fed to us – and trying to see the real world around us. I've gotten pretty good at dissecting AstroTurf and the narratives fed to the public and press." Will Rahn is the network's managing editor of politics and a CBS digital political correspondent, who wrote a commentary admitting the over the top, ridiculous, bias in favor of Hillary.[2] He wrote that "It shouldn't come as a surprise to anyone that, with a few exceptions, we were all tacitly or explicitly #WithHer, which has led to a certain anguish in the face of Donald Trump's victory. More than that, and more importantly, we also missed the story, after having spent months mocking the people who had a better sense of what was going on. This is all symptomatic of modern journalism's great moral and intellectual failing: its unbearable smugness. Had Hillary Clinton won, there'd be a winking 'we did it' feeling in the press, a sense that we were brave and called Trump a liar and saved the republic."

The National Broadcasting Company, NBC, is part of NBC Universal, which is part of Comcast. NBC hosted the first Presidential debate between Hillary Clinton and, now, President Donald J Trump. The debate was in late September and was moderated by Lester Holt. Holt proceeded to aggressively interrupt Trump an incredible 41 times. He passively and politely interrupted Hillary only seven times. This debate was insanely ridiculous and was almost unwatchable. Lester Holt falsely accused Trump of supporting the Iraq War, which was not true. Holt, not surprisingly, failed to even mention Benghazi. Did he ask Hillary about her e-mail controversy? Of course, he didn't. Did he ask her about the Clinton Foundation corruption or about the foundation taking money from governments hostile to the United States? Better chance of snow in Florida in August. Did he ask Hillary about her comments of referring to black people as "super predators"? No. Did he ask her about her praise of her 'friend and mentor', Robert Byrd (a former KKK member and recruiter)? Nope. Did he ask Trump about tax returns? Absolutely.[3] Did he bring up the issue of "Stop-and-frisk" to put Trump in a bad light? Yes, he certainly did. Did he bring up the so-called "birther" thing in an effort to cast Trump as a racist? Was there ever any doubt? This debate was a joke, but then again, so is NBC.

But when it comes to television Propaganda, CNN is King. They are truly the 'Fake News' Champions. There are rumors that CNN could be sold off because it weighs down its ownership's stock, Time Warner. Time Warner also has connections to the Council on Foreign Relations, the IMF, and other globalist entities.[4] I certainly hope CNN does get sold off and maybe replaced by people who don't actively work against the American people. It's people like CNN, the Clinton News Network, who actively help foment violence against the police by pushing lies. In 2015 there was an attack on the Dallas police headquarters and CNN host Fredricka Whitfield called the criminal, James Boulware, "courageous and brave, if not crazy." Their social justice agenda and propaganda put our police at risk, and that's not fair. CNN also hurts our country's reputation with their lies and hatred like when they fail to call out Obama on Anti-Israel policies for example. Of course, we all know they fed questions to Hillary, directly. Donna Brazile, the former DNC chair, and CNN contributor literally just gave the questions to the Clinton campaign in advance.[5] WikiLeaks documents unveiled how Brazile sent the Clinton campaign an email which said, "One of the questions directed to HRC tomorrow is from a woman with a rash," and this was the night before the CNN primary debate in Flint, Michigan in March. "Her family has lead poison and she will ask what, if anything, will Hillary do as president to help the ppl of Flint," Donna Brazile wrote in the email.[6] Absolutely Disgusting corruption and bias.

Anderson Cooper's Presidential debate performance was just sad. He was openly hostile to Trump and told the crowd to be quiet when they cheered for him. After the election was over, and Hillary and CNN lost, CNN continued its divineness and racism. CNN commentator, Van Jones, referred to the election results as a "Whitelash." His suggestion, of course, was that all Trump supporters are racist and they only supported President Donald J Trump because of skin color. CNN's racist commentator Marc Lamont Hill even went so far as to call black people who support President Trump as "mediocre negroes." What a vile statement.

Many major media outlets have admitted their extreme bias.[7] The propaganda media isn't limited to television. It also includes repulsive newspapers like the New York Times and The Washington Post. The New York Times, NYT, is primarily owned by the Mexican mega-billionaire, Carlos Slim. The Times is an elitist and utterly disgusting newspaper. They are totally disconnected from working-class and middle-class Americans. It goes without saying they were against Trump the entire time. New York Times Mediator Jim Rutenberg even admitted that the media missed everything by entirely ignoring what Trump supporters had to say and writing us off.[8] He wrote in an article after the election that:

> "The misfire on Tuesday night was about a lot more than a failure in polling. It was a failure to capture the boiling anger of a large portion of the American electorate that feels left behind by a selective recovery, betrayed by trade deals that they see as threats to their jobs and disrespected by establishment Washington, Wall Street, and the mainstream media. Journalists didn't question the polling data when it confirmed

their gut feeling that Mr. Trump could never in a million years pull it off. They portrayed Trump supporters who still believed he had a shot as being out of touch with reality. In the end, it was the other way around."

The media didn't just miss the story. They were the villains of it. One sick and disgusting individual, Ross Douthat, a columnist for the New York Times, joked about the assassination of Donald Trump in early 2016. He tweeted "Good news guys I've figured out how the Trump campaign ends" Douthat added a link to a YouTube video which depicts the assassination attempt of a fictional presidential candidate. What a repugnant, hateful, and sick creature this columnist is.

The Washington Post is owned by Jeff Bezos, who is on his way to becoming the richest man in the world. Bezos is the founder and CEO of Amazon and has a net worth of over $84 Billion Dollars. The Washington Post loves to oppose President Trump continually and they like to complain about what they deem to be conflicts of interest. But what about Jeff Bezos's Conflicts of Interest? What about the conflicts of interest of Jeff Bezos having $84 Billion Dollars and having the Washington Post attack President Trump? Maybe The Washington Post should do more articles about that rather than trying to attack the first President in my lifetime that I actually like, respect, support, helped to elect, am proud of, and is the most intelligent and courageous president of my lifetime and it's not even close.

There are also social media companies who are acting as propagandists. Twitter bans people who are not politically correct, like Milo Yiannopoulos. YouTube restricts and uses censorship against conservatives who they disagree with. Facebook, led by Mark Zuckerberg, is going down a Chinese-style propaganda route. The ACLU also supports Zuckerberg's censorship.[9] Google, another monopoly, helped fund Obama and Hillary and is obviously biased when it comes to being transparent on political issues. Who knows what Google is up to behind the scenes, using sophisticated algorithms to suppress news they dislike and promote the news which will hurt their opponents. Google has too much power, just like so many of the monopolies in our country. Google has decided to increase its banning efforts on what they decide is 'fake news.' Google has permanently banned 200 online publishers. The crackdown has started. In January 2017, Zerohedge.com had an article entitled: **Google Permanently Bans 200 "Fake News" Sites.**[10] In the article, it is explained that in total, Google took down 1.7 billion ads which they found to be in violation of their policies in 2016, which was more than double the 780 million they removed the year prior. I am reminded of the "Countering Disinformation And Propaganda Act" signed into law by Obama just before he left.

I think it's essential to actually have free speech in America. That's why we need to continue the conversation about making Free Speech a reality in our country! It's paramount to call out these propagandists that would limit our freedom of expression. It's very straightforward, use it or lose it. When you've got a 'Woman's March' that gets hours of coverage and Madonna threatens to blow up the Whitehouse, but the 'March for Life' gets less than 1% of the same coverage, it's ridiculous. Let's stand up for the first amendment that so many Patriots have died for and that our Founding Fathers cherished.

Six

CIA

The Central Intelligence Agency has a history that many people are not aware of or chose not to talk about. There is no doubt, very patriotic, America-Loving, brave, people who have served and continue to serve in the agency, and this does not reflect on those individuals. This is about the more globalist, shady, rogue, criminal elements within the agency and their crimes in America and around the world.

In this chapter, we will discuss the history of the Central Intelligence Agency, starting with its inception. We'll examine operations like 'Radio Free Europe,' 'Operation Mockingbird', and 'Project MKUltra.' We'll talk about the agency's activities in various Central and South American countries, and the overview of the 'The Church Committee' in the 1970's. Finally, we'll discuss ways we can improve our Country's intelligence gathering processes in a way that has proper oversight, does not recklessly destabilize governments around the world (helping keep us in endless wars), and that respects the civil liberties of American citizens.

The Central Intelligence Agency was officially created in 1947 under the National Security Act of 1947.[1] The National Security Council, NSC was created as well. The Central Intelligence Agency was given enormous amounts of power and was responsible for advising the NSC on intelligence-related affairs. The CIA's original purpose was to only gather information about foreign governments. It was against the law for the CIA to collect intelligence and have intelligence operations on American soil, (a law which has not been properly respected throughout the CIA's history as we'll discuss). It was a time after the second World War. Tens of millions of people around the world were dead from the war. People were afraid and tired of war. The dangers from the formidable Soviet Union were very present. President Truman created the Central Intelligence Group (CIG) in 1946 to perform secret activities and to help warn the government about threats. Many in the government wanted expanded Intelligence operations. When the National Security Act of 1947 was passed, the CIG was dissolved, and the CIA was formed. The CIA was responsible for organizing America's Intelligence gathering efforts and searching for Intelligence related to overall national security concerns.[2] The CIA answered to the National Security Council and to the President directly, both of whom would give directives for the CIA to follow. There was also a position called the Director of Central Intelligence (DCI). The DCI's job was to be the head of the CIA and head of the intelligence community, protect intelligence sources and techniques, and advise the President on Intelligence matters. In 1949 the CIA obtained, even more, power when the Central Intelligence Agency Act was passed. The CIA was free from any of the usual limitations on funding. CIA funding could now come from other departments and be transferred in a way with no restrictions what so ever. The CIA's total budget was kept secret and remained highly confidential.

In 1949 the CIA started its first big and serious propaganda fountain called Radio Free Europe. Radio Free Europe was an effort to combat communism in certain strategic locations of the world. After WWII had ended, the big threat was then communism. Hitler was defeated, but thousands of ex-Nazis came to the United States. Many of these ex-Nazis were recruited by the FBI and the CIA to get intelligence on the Soviet Union. Other ex-Nazi scientists were used to try and advance technology against the Soviets. The Second World War was over, but the Cold War was just beginning, and one of the ways you compete in this war, if you're the CIA, is through propaganda outlets such as Radio Free Europe. The CIA used an anti-communist front group called the National Committee for a Free Europe, NCFE, founded by Allen Dulles. Radio Free Europe grew out of the NCFE and eventually gained tremendous support from President Dwight D. Eisenhower's 'Crusade for Freedom' campaign. The Crusade for Freedom raised money for Radio Free Europe. It inspired Americans to donate their "Truth Dollars" for the cause. The United States wanted to fight back against the communist appeal to Europe's intellectuals. The Cold War was a political war. The battle was a psychological struggle. It was fought through efforts such as RFE. In 1950, RFE started to build a large international broadcasting staff. Journalists were hired for every language, and a complicated intelligence gathering operation gave RFE important broadcast material. Radio Free Europe also surveilled Communist publications and radio activities so they would know what information to use to counter with. The truth is that Communism has killed hundreds of millions of people around the world throughout history. It's hard to hold it against the CIA for wanting to win the Cold War, promote freedom, and defeat the Soviets. It's what came next that is truly terrifying.

Robert Penn Warren was an American poet and novelist who said: "History cannot give us a program for the future, but it can give us a fuller understanding of ourselves, and of our common humanity, so that we can better face the future." He also said, "The lack of a sense of history is the damnation of the modern world." I think these quotes are important for people who believe anything they hear from propaganda media. During the Cold War, the CIA didn't just have propaganda outlets in Europe, it also created them in America as well. The Central Intelligence Agency created a new propaganda operation here domestically in the United States, called 'Operation Mockingbird.' Operation Mockingbird was a secret project where the CIA would purchase enormous media influence behind the scenes at major media outlets and news networks. They would also put reporters directly on the payroll of the CIA.[3] It was called Operation 'Mockingbird' because in the wild mockingbirds will only repeat what they hear and mimic other sounds in nature. Eventually, the media assets will include over 25 organizations and more than 400 journalists by the CIA's own confession. Media owners were easy to control and would be fearful of going against the government. Many times it was about just ignoring big stories. In the book 'Fooling America', by Robert Parry, Parry says that, "The people who succeeded and did well were those who didn't stand up, who didn't write the big stories, who looked the other way when history was happening in front of them, and went along either consciously or just by cowardice with the deception of the American people." The CIA had far exceeded its original intention with Operation Mockingbird and was acting as an unelected government. In the book 'Propaganda' written by Edward Bernays in 1928, Bernays wrote that "The conscious and intelligent manipulation of the organized habits and opinions of the masses is an important element in democratic society. Those who manipulate this unseen mechanism of society constitute an invisible government which is the true ruling power of our country. ...We are governed, our minds are molded, our tastes formed, our ideas suggested, largely by men we have never heard of. This is a logical result of the way in which our democratic society is organized. Vast numbers of human beings must cooperate in this manner if they are to live together as a smoothly functioning society. ...In almost every act of our daily lives, whether in the sphere of politics or business, in our social conduct or our ethical thinking, we are dominated by the relatively small number of persons...who understand the mental processes and social patterns of the masses. It is they who pull the wires which control the public mind."

Project MK-ULTRA started in the 1950's, which experimented with mind control on people illegally. The Scientific Intelligence Division and the U.S. Army's Chemical Corps were largely involved. The United Stated Supreme Court eventually stated that MK-ULTRA's aim was to find "the research and development of chemical, biological, and radiological materials capable of employment in clandestine operations to control human behavior." The Project used a wide variety of methods to manipulate people's behavior such verbal abuse, sexual assault, isolation, hypnosis, sensory deprivation, and especially using drugs. One of the primary drugs they used was LSD (Lysergic acid diethylamide), aka Acid, which causes hallucinations, anxiety, fear, paranoia, panic attacks, pupil dilation, heart rate increase, and extreme/rapid shifts in cognitive thought. Research also shows that the drug causes people to be more suggestible when they are under its effect. MK-ULTRA was widespread, and Congress grew concerned. Investigations were thwarted because CIA Director, Richard Helms, ordered for all MK-ULTRA files to be destroyed in 1973.

The CIA becomes very involved in Central and South America. As the decades passed, the Agency interfered with countries like Guatemala, Haiti, the Dominican Republic, Ecuador, Brazil, Bolivia, Chile, El Salvador, Panama, and Honduras just to name a few. Central and South America became the playground of the CIA. Activities included overthrowing democratically elected leaders, installing puppet regimes (many of whom kill and brutalize their own people), training death squads, drug trafficking, and much worse.

Domestically, the CIA's spying on American citizens goes to new levels with Operation CHAOS. President Lyndon Johnson wants the Central Intelligence Agency to have its own investigations on issues relating to domestic dissent in 1965. CIA Agents work undercover, posing as students to disrupt campus organizations that are protesting the war in Vietnam. Operation CHAOS ends up spying on thousands of individuals and many organizations.

As the CIA's list of crimes started getting longer and longer, public outrage pressures Congress to hold hearings on CIA crimes in 1975.[4] Senator Frank Church leads the Senate investigation in what is known as "The Church Committee." The official name was the 'United States Senate Select Committee to Study Governmental Operations with Respect to Intelligence Activities.'[5] The following is an excerpt from the:

FINAL REPORT OF THE SELECT COMMITTEE TO STUDY GOVERNMENTAL OPERATIONS WITH RESPECT TO INTELLIGENCE ACTIVITIES
UNITED STATES SENATE
(starting on page 96)
"*Foreign Intelligence and Domestic Dissent*
In the late 1960's, CIA and NSA, acting in response to presidential pressure, turned their technological capacity and great resources to- ward spying on certain Americans. The initial impetus was to deter- mine whether the antiwar move-ment-and to a lesser extent the "black power" movement-were controlled by foreigners. Despite evidence that there was no significant foreign influence, the intelligence gathering which culminated in CIA's "Operation CHAOS" followed

the general pattern of broadening in scope and intensity. The procedure for one aspect of these programs was established by an informal agreement between the CIA and FBI in 1966, which permitted CIA to engage in "internal security" activities in the United States.

a. Origins of CIA Involvement in "Internal Security Functions"

The National Security Act of 1947 explicitly prohibited the CIA from exercising "police, subpoena, or law-enforcement powers, or internal security functions." But the Act did not address the question of the CIA's authority to conduct clandestine intelligence activity within the United States for what Secretary Forrestal called "purposes outside of this country."

Under Director Hoover, the FBI interpreted the term "internal security functions" broadly to encompass almost "anything that CIA might be doing in the United States." 436 Throughout the 1950's and into the early 1960's, Director Hoover's position led to jurisdictional conflicts between the CIA and the FBI.

The Bureau insisted on being informed of the CIA's activity in the United States so that it could be coordinated with the Bureau. As the FBI liaison with the CIA in that period recalled, "CIA would take action, it would come to our attention and we would have a flap."

In 1966 the FBI and CIA negotiated an informal agreement to regularize their coordination. This agreement was said to have "led to a great improvement" and almost eliminated the "flaps."

Under the agreement, the CIA would "seek concurrence and coordination of the FBI" before engaging in clandestine activity in the United States and the FBI would "concur and coordinate if the pro- posed action does not conflict with any operation, current or planned, including active investigation of the FBI." When an operative recruited by the CIA abroad arrived in the United States, the FBI would "be advised" and the two agencies would "confer regarding the handling of the agent in the United States." The CIA would continue its "handling" of the agent for "foreign intelligence" purposes. The FBI would also become involved where there were "internal security factors," although it was recognized that the CIA might continue to "handle" the agent in the United States and provide the Bureau with "information" bearing on "internal security matters.

As part of their handling of "internal security factors," CIA operatives were used after 1966 to report on domestic "dissidents" for the FBI. There were infrequent instances in which, according to the former FBI liaison with CIA:

CIA had penetrations abroad in radical, revolutionary organizations and the individual was coming here to attend a conference, a meeting, and would be associating with leading dissidents, and the question came up, can he be of any use to us, can we have access to him during that period. In most instances, because he was here for a relatively short period, we would levy the requirement or the request upon the CIA to find out what was taking place at the meetings to get his assessment of the individuals that he was meeting, and any other general intelligence that he could collect from his associations with the people who were of interest to us.

The policies embodied in the 1966 agreement and the practice under it clearly involved the CIA in the performance of "internal security functions." At no time did the Executive branch ask Congress to amend the 1947 act to modify its ban against CIA exercising "internal security functions." Nor was Congress asked to clarify the ambiguity of the 1947 act about the CIA's authority to conduct clandestine foreign intelligence and counterintelligence activities within the United States, a matter dealt with even today by Executive Order.

Moreover, National Security Council Intelligence Directive 5 provided authority within the Executive Branch for the Director of Central Intelligence to coordinate, and for the CIA to conduct, counterintelligence activities abroad to protect the United States against not only espionage and sabotage, but also "subversion." However, NSCID 5 did not purport to give the CIA authority for counterintelligence activities in the United States, as provided in the FBICIA agreement of 1966."

The Church Committee also discussed the assassination of President John F. Kennedy.[6] The following is an excerpt from the final report of the "THE INVESTIGATION OF THE ASSASSINATION OF PRESIDENT JOHN F. KENNEDY: PERFORMANCE OF THE INTELLIGENCE AGENCIES" (starting on page 23):

"III. THE UNITED STATES GOVERNMENT RESPONSE TO THE ASSASSINATION: NOVEMBER 22, 1963 TO JANUARY 1, 1964
This section of the Report discusses the performance of the FBI and the CIA during the weeks immediately following the assassination of President John F. Kennedy.

The performance of these agencies should not be evaluated in isolation. Senior government officials, both within the agencies and outside them, wanted the investigation completed promptly and all conspiracy rumors dispelled. For example, only three days after the assassination, Deputy Attorney General Nicholas Katzenbach wrote Presidential Assistant Bill Moyers:

It is important that all of the facts surrounding President Kennedy's assassination be made public in a way which will satisfy people in the United States and abroad that all the facts have been told and that a statement to this effect be made now.

1. The public must be satisfied that Oswald was the assassin; that he did not have confederates who are still at large; and that the evidence was such that he would have been convicted -at trial.
2. Speculation about Oswald's motivation ought to be cut off, and we should have some basis for rebutting thought that this was a Communist conspiracy or (as the Iron Curtain press is saying) a right-wing conspiracy to blame it on the Communists.

On November 29, 1963, President Johnson told Director Hoover that, although he wanted to "get by" on just the FBI report, the only way to stop the "rash of investigations" was to appoint a high-level committee to evaluate that report.2 On December 9, 1963, Deputy Attorney General Katzenbach wrote each member of the Warren Commission recommending that the Commission immediately issue a press release stating that the FBI report clearly showed there was no international conspiracy, and that Oswald was a loner.

A.   The CIA Response

This section deals with the CIA's immediate response in investigating the assassination. It discusses what information the CIA received alleging Cuban involvement in the assassination, and the steps taken by the Agency to investigate those allegations.

Since Oswald had come to the attention of the CIA in October and November 1963, the Agency needed no orders to begin an investigation of the assassination. On November 8, the CIA received an FBI report dated October 31, 1963, discussing the Bureau's investigation of Oswald's activities in New Orleans. On November 15, that report was forwarded to SAS Counterintelligence, the CIA section specializing in Cuban affairs. The routing slip on the report indicates it was sent to the Counterintelligence Division of the CIA on November 22. The Chief of SAS Counterintelligence recalled that immediately after the assassination, Director McCone requested all Agency material on Oswald. The Chief testified that he probably reported seeing a recent FBI report on Oswald, but he could not remember whether SAS had routed the report to the Counterintelligence Division before or after the assassination.

The CIA Mexico Station also realized that Lee Harvey Oswald had come to its attention in early October and cabled CIA Headquarters at 5:00 p.m. on the afternoon of the assassination. Other CIA stations and overseas elements of the State Department and Defense Department soon began reporting any information they received which might be relevant to the assassination.

For the first twenty-four hours after the assassination, the CIA's attention focused primarily on Oswald's September 27, 1963, visit to Mexico City. CIA Headquarters wanted all relevant information developed by its Mexico Station in order to begin its analysis of the information. On the morning of November 23, Director McCone met with President Johnson and his national security advisor, McGeorge Bundy, to brief them on the information CIA Headquarters had received from its Mexico Station. McCone's memorandum for the record of that meeting contains the essential information extracted from the Mexico Station's cable which had been received by that time."

There was an Iran hostage crisis in 1979 where 52 American citizens were taken, hostage. The crisis goes on for 444 days, spanning from November 4, 1979, all the way to January 20, 1981. Then there was the collapse and fall of the Soviet Union in 1991. The Central Intelligence Agency fails to predict the single most significant point of the Cold War. The CIA by that point had gotten so far removed from its original purpose they couldn't see the collapse coming.

Many believe that the CIA should be abolished. It has far exceeded its bounds endless times throughout its history. Who has the CIA benefited over the years? Has it benefited the American people? Has it benefited our national security interests or have certain elements of the Agency enriched themselves at any cost? We should have a conversation in our country about the civil liberties of Americans and the proper role of Intelligence gathering in our nation. The Great Dr. Ron Paul said that "Real Patriotism is a willingness to challenge the government when it's wrong."

Seven

CHINA

In this chapter, we will discuss how China has hurt the American people, damaged our economy, and its role in promoting globalism around the world. We'll start by exploring China's history of communism which began in the 20ᵗʰ Century and has dominated it ever since. We'll study the life and rise to power of Mao Zedong, aka Chairman Mao, who was the number one mass murderer in history. After that, we'll examine the lack of freedoms in China, including internet censorship. Next, I'll make the case as for why China joining the World Trade Organization in 2001 was an absolute catastrophe. Then, we'll investigate China, including negative effects of their currency manipulation, the stealing natural resources around the world, and how it has no environmental standards of any kind. Finally, we'll discuss what China has been up to recently including its interests in the American entertainment industry, aggressively expanding in the South China Sea, and its President, Xi Jinping, promoting Globalism.

The twentieth century was extremely brutal for China. It started immediately with a bunch of civil unrest, economic instability, political turmoil, civil wars, world war two, famine, and massive human suffering. The Communist Party of China was founded in 1921. Marxist ideas were starting to spread around China like wildfire. The party name was called 'Zhōngguó Gòngchǎn Dǎng' which just means Chinese Communist Party. It had about 60 members initially when it was officially declared. As the communists grew in number, they eventually collided with Chiang Kai-shek. Chiang Kai-shek was socially conservative and promoted older, more traditional Chinese cultural values. He rejected Western democracies and was authoritarian, but he also despised the communists in his own country. He killed and imprisoned many of them. The communists created a plethora of 'Soviet Areas' where they armed themselves. Chiang Kai-shek was successful in driving the 'Red Army' out of their bases, which started what is now known as the 'Long March.' The Long March was the military retreat by the Red Army (of the CPC) where they fled from South China to the Northern and Western parts of the country. It was at this time that the defeated Chinese communists had to start rethinking their policies and plans for obtaining more power and control. It was then that Mao Zedong started his ascent to power, and would eventually go on to be the largest mass murderer in the history of the world.

Mao Zedong was born in 1893 in Shaoshan in the Hunan Province, China. His family were farmers, and his disciplinarian father was one of the wealthier farmers in Shaoshan. Mao worked on his father's farm but was interested in history and read as much as he could. China was a futile society and life was very brutal. By the time he was 13 years old, he was already working full-time on the family farm. He lacked a real education, but still had a great ambition in life. Eventually, in his 20's Mao became an assistant in the Beijing Library and was mocked by the average students. It was at this point when Mao Zedong became a revolutionary. He also became a member of the Communist Party and started preaching communism to the peasants.

The following is an excerpt from the 'Manifesto of the Communist Party by Karl Marx and Frederick Engels February 1848' (II. Proletarians and Communists):

"The proletariat will use its political supremacy to wrest, by degree, all capital from the bourgeoisie, to centralize all instruments of production in the hands of the State, i.e., of the proletariat organized as the ruling class; and to increase the total productive forces as rapidly as possible.

Of course, in the beginning, this cannot be effected except by means of despotic inroads on the rights of property, and on the conditions of bourgeois production; by means of measures, therefore, which appear economically insufficient and untenable, but which, in the course of the movement, outstrip themselves, necessitate further inroads upon the old social order, and are unavoidable as a means of entirely revolutionising the mode of production.

These measures will, of course, be different in different countries.

Nevertheless, in most advanced countries, the following will be pretty generally applicable.

1. Abolition of property in land and application of all rents of land to public purposes.
2. A heavy progressive or graduated income tax.
3. Abolition of all rights of inheritance.
4. Confiscation of the property of all emigrants and rebels.
5. Centralisation of credit in the hands of the state, by means of a national bank with State capital and an exclusive monopoly.

6. Centralisation of the means of communication and transport in the hands of the State.

7. Extension of factories and instruments of production owned by the State; the bringing into cultivation of waste-lands, and the improvement of the soil generally in accordance with a common plan.

8. Equal liability of all to work. Establishment of industrial armies, especially for agriculture.

9. Combination of agriculture with manufacturing industries; gradual abolition of all the distinction between town and country by a more equable distribution of the populace over the country.

10. Free education for all children in public schools. Abolition of children's factory labor in its present form. Combination of education with industrial production, &c, &c.

When, in the course of development, class distinctions have disappeared, and all production has been concentrated in the hands of a vast association of the whole nation, the public power will lose its political character. Political power, properly so called, is merely the organized power of one class for oppressing another. If the proletariat during its contest with the bourgeoisie is compelled, by the force of circumstances, to organise itself as a class, if, by means of a revolution, it makes itself the ruling class, and, as such, sweeps away by force the old conditions of production, then it will, along with these conditions, have swept away the conditions for the existence of class antagonisms and of classes generally, and will thereby have abolished its own supremacy as a class.

In place of the old bourgeois society, with its classes and class antagonisms, we shall have an association, in which the free development of each is the condition for the free development of all."

This was the time in China when communism and Marxist ideas were rising rapidly. Chiang Kai-shek then began fighting back as we discussed earlier, and this escalated and eventually led to a major Communist defeat where they started the Long March in retreat. During this March Mao became the unquestioned leader of the Chinese communist rebels. Speaking about the battle against Chiang Kai-shek's government, Mao said "Revolution is not a dinner party, nor an essay, nor a painting, nor a piece of embroidery; it cannot be so refined, so leisurely and gentle, so temperate, kind, courteous, restrained and magnanimous. A revolution is an insurrection, an act of violence by which one class overthrows another."[1] He also spoke about his general strategy saying "The enemy advances, we retreat; the enemy camps, we harass; the enemy tires, we attack; the enemy retreats, we pursue."[2] During the Long March, tens of thousands of the communists died, and very few remained. Those that survived eventually ended up Yan'an, a remote and isolated location where they were safe. It was here in Yan'an where the center of the Chinese Communist revolution would be located. They would regain support and bolster their numbers once again. Right when Chiang Kai-shek's forces started to catch up for another confrontation, something unexpected happened. Imperial Japan invaded China and started killing the Chinese people and conquering vast areas of the country. The Nanking Massacre was just one incident that left hundreds of thousands of Chinese dead. Mao Zedong and Chiang Kai-shek were forced to put their civil war on hold, temporarily, to work together to defeat the Japanese invaders. An anti-Japanese alliance was made. World War II was about to begin. America eventually sent aid to help Mao fight against the Japanese since they were mutual enemies. After the war was over, the communists, with American help, had become more dangerous, better equipped, better trained, and stronger than ever before. The civil war was then able to be resumed for a few years. The communists were successful. By this point, Mao had already become the chairman of the Central Committee of the Communist Party of China and on October 1, 1949, Mao Zedong officially created the People's Republic of China (PRC) in Beijing.[3] Over 30 years of civil war (and war in general) had come to an end, but the real suffering for the Chinese people was just about to begin. As the authoritarian dictator of China, Mao would not only continue to follow the guiding principles of communism and Marxism, but he would expand on them and get even more hardcore, creating what is known as "Maoism."

Here are some of the original 'Principles of Communism' listed in "Manifesto of the Communist Party" by Karl Marx and Frederick Engels February 1848':

"The Principles of Communism

– 1 –
What is Communism?
Communism is the doctrine of the conditions of the liberation of the proletariat.

– 2 –
What is the proletariat?
The proletariat is that class in society which lives entirely from the sale of its labor and does not draw profit from any kind of capital; whose weal and woe, whose life and death,

whose sole existence depends on the demand for labor – hence, on the changing state of business, on the vagaries of unbridled competition. The proletariat, or the class of proletarians, is, in a word, the working class of the 19th century.

– 14 –

What will this new social order have to be like?

Above all, it will have to take the control of industry and of all branches of production out of the hands of mutually competing individuals, and instead institute a system in which all these branches of production are operated by society as a whole – that is, for the common account, according to a common plan, and with the participation of all members of society. It will, in other words, abolish competition and replace it with association. Moreover, since the management of industry by individuals necessarily implies private property, and since competition is in reality merely the manner and form in which the control of industry by private property owners expresses itself, it follows that private property cannot be separated from competition and the individual management of industry. Private property must, therefore, be abolished and in its place must come the common utilization of all instruments of production and the distribution of all products according to common agreement – in a word, what is called the communal ownership of goods. In fact, the abolition of private property is, doubtless, the shortest and most significant way to characterize the revolution in the whole social order which has been made necessary by the development of industry – and for this reason it is rightly advanced by communists as their main demand.

– 18 –
What will be the course of this revolution?

The main measures, emerging as the necessary result of existing relations, are the following:

(i) Limitation of private property through progressive taxation, heavy inheritance taxes, abolition of inheritance through collateral lines (brothers, nephews, etc.) forced loans, etc.

(ii) Gradual expropriation of landowners, industrialists, railroad magnates and shipowners, partly through competition by state industry, partly directly through compensation in the form of bonds.

(iii) Confiscation of the possessions of all emigrants and rebels against the majority of the people.

(iv) Organization of labor or employment of proletarians on publicly owned land, in factories and workshops, with competition among the workers being abolished and with the factory owners, in so far as they still exist, being obliged to pay the same high wages as those paid by the state.

(v) An equal obligation on all members of society to work until such time as private property has been completely abolished. Formation of industrial armies, especially for agriculture.

(vi) Centralization of money and credit in the hands of the state through a national bank with state capital, and the suppression of all private banks and bankers.

(vii) Increase in the number of national factories, workshops, railroads, ships; bringing new lands into cultivation and improvement of land already under cultivation – all in proportion to the growth of the capital and labor force at the disposal of the nation.

(viii) Education of all children, from the moment they can leave their mother's care, in national establishments at national cost. Education and production together.

(ix) Construction, on public lands, of great palaces as communal dwellings for associated groups of citizens engaged in both industry and agriculture and combining in their way of life the advantages of urban and rural conditions while avoiding the one-sidedness and drawbacks of each.

(x) Destruction of all unhealthy and jerry-built dwellings in urban districts.

(xi) Equal inheritance rights for children born in and out of wedlock.

(xii) Concentration of all means of transportation in the hands of the nation.

It is impossible, of course, to carry out all these measures at once. But one will always bring others in its wake. Once the first radical attack on private property has been launched, the proletariat will find itself forced to go ever further, to concentrate increasingly in the hands of the state all capital, all agriculture, all transport, all trade. All the foregoing measures are directed to this end; and they will become practicable and feasible, capable of producing their centralizing effects to precisely the degree that the proletariat, through its labor, multiplies the country's productive forces. Finally, when all capital, all production, all exchange have been brought together in the hands of the nation, private property will disappear of its own accord, money will become superfluous, and production will so expand and man so change that society will be able to slough off whatever of its old economic habits may remain."

As Mao Zedong was now in full and total control of China, the hellish nightmare for the Chinese people would start to intensify, even though millions worshiped him as some type of god (and continue to worship him to this day). The land was stolen and redistributed. Land Lords were killed and publically laughed at. Those who were critical of Mao or the Communist party were violently destroyed. Intellectuals, students, competing politicians, and anyone else opposed to Mao or even critical of him were labeled "rightists." Mao launched an "anti-Rightist" campaign. They lost their jobs. Tens of thousands were sent directly to prison camps. Millions were killed. Newspapers were censored and shut down. The writers were harassed, beaten, and threatened. The "Anti-Rightist Purge" destroyed millions of families. Mao Zedong got even more disconnected from reality. He became paranoid which only fueled his murderous instincts. People could even be labeled a "rightist" for scratching their head the wrong way or even just looking suspicious. In 1958, Mao launched a program that was called the "Great Leap Forward." The means of food production and agriculture were collectivized, and government operated. Hundreds of millions of peasants were put to work on collective farms. Grain output was expected to increase massively. What actually happened was colossal famine.

Entire villages died of starvation. The program also had peasants produce immense amounts of steel that was utterly useless. The people were left with nothing. They had to eat grass, tree bark, and farm animals. When those things were all gone, widespread cannibalism took place. The Chinese ate the bodies of the recently dead. Historians have a difficult time estimating just how bad the cannibalism got. It was the worst man-made famine in history. Tens of millions were dead, and if you calculate the deaths after Mao Zedong's death, from

Chinese Communism after that, which was so pushed by Mao, its hundreds of millions who died as a result of his failed communist policies. Mao Zedong finally died in 1976. Here are a few Mao Zedong quotes which further illustrate what an evil monster he really was.[4]

"Communism is not love. Communism is a hammer which we use to crush the enemy."

"Genuine equality between the sexes can only be realized in the process of the socialist transformation of society as a whole." (Ironic since Mao was a famous philanderer and womanizer)

"Political power grows out of the barrel of a gun."

"To read too many books is harmful."

"Passivity is fatal to us. Our goal is to make the enemy passive."

"There is a serious tendency toward capitalism among the well-to-do peasants."

Many Maoist, Communist leaders have continued running China ever since Mao's death, and as a result, the Chinese people have continued to be slaves. China continues as an authoritarian regime to this day. It is a country that still restricts political freedom, free expression, religious liberty, controls a rigged economy, and violates fundamental human rights. It also monitors and controls free speech in general and has a tight grip on the Internet. Imprisonment of political opponents is very much standard practice in China. The Chinese Communist Party has absolute power over the country's politics. Political opponents are viewed as nothing more than domestic threats that need to be dealt with and silenced. The Government uses brute force and justifies this authoritarianism by claiming it's in the national interest. They claim it's about keeping the country safe from instability, but really it's opponent dominating political opponents.

The state also restricts any and all religious freedoms which they deem to be not normal. An article by the 'Human Rights Watch' explained how the Chinese government took away 150 crosses from Christian churches in the Zhejiang Province in the 2013-2014 time span alone. Buddhists and other groups are also targeted. During that same time, a Buddhist leader named Wu Zeheng was detained along with many of his followers and no legal reason was given for doing so. This sort of thing happens all the time. They classify many religious groups that are not under their control as evil cults and threats. Falun Gong is a spiritual/meditation practice which has been viciously attacked and persecuted as well. The government also expels thousands of foreign missionaries.

All Chinese media are subject to incredibly powerful censorship and governmental controls. Before official press cards are issued, Chinese journalists have to take political ideology exams. Television news networks, radio stations, and film producers are given directives by the State Administration of Press Publication.

Internet Censorship is over the top and extreme. China has a population of over 1.357 billion people, so naturally, controlling the flow of information is paramount for the communists. Its internet is controlled publically, by the government. China has one of the strongest and most sophisticated censorship systems in the world. Thousands of websites are blocked by the communist party government on a wide array of topics but especially anything which could potentially challenge the political establishment there. The number of internet users in China is estimated to be about 700,000,000. In 2015 the Chinese government completed a two-year project to dramatically build out the country's core internet infrastructure. There is also a Chinese 'Internet Police' force of millions that the government uses. They go after critical opinion, monitor online chat rooms, and read text messages which citizens send. It is referred to as the "Great Firewall of China".[5] One of the many things censored, for example, is information about the 'Tiananmen Square Massacre' from more than a quarter of a century ago. The term "Tiananmen Square" is censored totally. Even words that are closely related or phrases similar to it get blocked. The date of the event (June 4, 1989) is blocked. Even the combination of the numbers 6, 4, 1989 is blocked.

The world's highest populated country is just not allowed to read information about the violent event like it has been absolutely erased from history. I think we as Americans should wake up to the fact that we are heading toward this type of communist style censorship of our internet access. YouTube, Google, Facebook, Twitter, and others all actively censoring speech they disagree with. We have to learn from history so that it's not repeated here in the United States of America.

In 2001, China was welcomed into the World Trade Organization, WTO. At the turn of the millennium in 2000, there were Washington insiders and elites who argued that there would be a boom in American exports to China. Their assessments could not have been more wrong. The result was an obviously huge drop-off in American manufacturing that we can all see. Factories were shut down all over the country. American workers suffered hellish conditions, not only from having to compete with Chinese imports but the high taxes from Obama on top of it. Not to mention the regulatory craziness. It was just one hit after another for the worker. People with once good middle class, family sustaining jobs were forced into low-wage part-time jobs. The welfare state has grown so enormous it's difficult to even know just how big it really is and all of the impacts it has. Taxes went up. Wages went down. Factories closed. We also lose hundreds of billions a year with China from the trade deficits. There is no debate. From every perspective, China joining the WTO has been absolutely incredibly hurtful to the United States of America.

President Trump has expressed interest in labeling China a "currency manipulator" which would be a great thing because that is exactly what they are. The way it works is, China buys a plethora of foreign currencies, especially the dollar, which pushes them higher against the Chinese yuan. China manipulates its way into getting any kind of global advantage it can. China "pegs" the yuan to an entire group of currencies that includes the dollar, using a fixed exchange rate. If the dollar loses value, the Chinese government goes in and buys dollars using the U.S. Treasury to give it support. The US debt to China is now well over a trillion dollars.

China also steals natural resources all over the world. For example, while our American soldiers fight in Afghanistan and die, China is busy extracting the rare earth minerals from the Country. We do the fighting and heavy lifting while they suck all the minerals and wealth out. Trillions of dollars in minerals just sitting there, especially Lithium. Lithium is used for cell phone batteries, nuclear components, laptops, toys, health products, and hundreds of other things. It's incredibly valuable. They also suck up resources in South America, Africa, and anywhere else where it's profitable for them. The environmental standards, domestically, are very horrifying in China. That's because there are none. Smog is so bad in Beijing you have to literally wear a mask.[6] There is wastewater that is dumped into the rivers, massive industrial pollution, and its soil is totally contaminated with all sorts of pollutants.

Hundreds of millions of people in China have no safe drinking water. This pollution spreads all over the world and affects all of us. Despite the fact that they have literally no standards of any kind, the Government still supports many of the Global/International entities which push for harsher environmental standards in America. The height of hypocrisy.

China has also been aggressively expanding in the South China Sea. China has been literally constructing artificial islands and expanding its naval military capabilities in waters that it should not be in.[7] This stress in the South China Sea could lead to an escalation, and it is time for China to realize its own extensive problems as a nation and stop expanding. But the South China Sea isn't the only place where they are expanding.

They're also developing in our own country, right in Hollywood. Wang Jianlin, a Chinese Billionaire, who also happens to be China's richest man wants to invest billions into Hollywood.[8] He has profound connections with the government and is very close to the CPC. The billionaire has said that he wants to "change the world where rules are set by foreigners." China intends to control the entertainment industry so that it can promote its own ideology over an American ideology. Of course Hollywood is more than happy to take money from Chinese investors. People with no soul will take money from anyone.

Recently, Chinese President Xi Jinping gave a speech at the World Economic Forum in Davos, Switzerland. This was globalism central. Xi declared himself as this ultimate globalist, and as a protector of globalist policies. His speech was all about globalism and how great he thinks it is, and how it should be spread around even more.[9] I think Xi should come to Pennsylvania, Ohio, Wisconsin, and Michigan and other places that have lost factories and wealth and he should talk to the American workers living in poverty about how great globalism is for them. He should tell Americans who can't afford their bills how great China is promoting failed globalist policies. It's time for us as Americans to regain control of our country and retake our own sovereignty. Nobody wants war with China, but we're certainly not going to be intimidated or bullied by this globalist, communist, hypocritical country.

Eight

HOLLYWOOD

I n this chapter, we will discuss the degrading, shameful, humiliating, divisive, hateful, and overall negative effect that the Entertainment Industry in the Western World, specifically Hollywood, has on society. We will discuss how violence and hateful rhetoric is promoted daily. We'll examine the 'Social Justice Warrior,' liberal, big government, globalist agenda that is so massively shoveled out of Hollywood and directed towards the masses. Then, we'll talk about the hypocrisy of celebrities and why they don't really care about the poor. After that, we'll investigate celebrities and their fascination with groups such as the Illuminati, their interest in Scientology, and ugly history of pedophilia in the entertainment industry. Next, we'll explore the vicious attacks on God, America, Christianity, masculinity, freedom, free markets, the Constitution, traditional values, the middle class, and fly over country. Finally, we'll discuss what we can do to boycott and peacefully fight back against Hollywood.

We've all watched action movies. We've all seen violence on television and in movies. It's good for ratings. It's good for the box office.

It's good for the bottom line. It's a captivating thing. It draws people in. They enjoy watching it, and Hollywood enjoys making money from it. Personally, I don't have a problem with it. It's their freedom of speech to make the films and shows they want. I don't believe in censorship like the government does. But what happens when celebrities start calling for violence in real life? What happens when they call for violence against President Trump? What happens when they support a domestic terrorist group like 'Black Lives Matter'? What happens when they spread fear and panic to such an extreme point, that thousands of their brain-dead zombie followers react in a violent way against Trump supporters? Nothing happens. We've glorified a culture where they are allowed to do whatever they want. They have power, fame, money, and influence. The double standard in our society is insane. In January 2017, at the Women's March on Washington, which was not about actually empowering women with freedom but was about promoting division in America, Madonna made an appearance. She threatened to blow up the White House. It was a direct threat against President Trump. Will she get in any trouble? Of course, not. Imagine if some guy in a cowboy hat had threatened to blow up the White House and it was a threat against President Hillary Clinton? He'd be locked up so fast. The Black lives matter group which rakes in tons of cash, including from George Soros, has threatened the lives of our Police. They create tremendous racial tensions and tensions between civilians and law enforcement. They say things like "What do we want? Dead Cops! When do we want them? Now!" and "Pigs in a blanket, fry em' like bacon!". It's an attack against civilization itself. It's an assault on the people that protect us from anarchy and chaos. There are many celebrities who support the domestic terrorist group, BLM, including: Jay-Z, Beyonce, Katy Perry, Justin Timberlake, Josh Groban, Kim Kardashian, Tyga, Kerry Washington, Lady Gaga, Jesse Williams, Rihanna, Olivia Wilde, Macklemore, LeBron James,

Mariah Carey, Lena Dunham, Trey Songz, Mark Zuckerberg, Hillary Clinton (If she can even be considered a celebrity with such small crowd sizes), and many others. The hateful and violent rhetoric is absolutely out of control. There have been endless death threats against President Trump. I'm so sick of it. Does the media hound these celebrities nonstop always making them denounce those threats? Nope. Remember the way they asked Trump to denounce the KKK like 75 Million times? Yet they don't ask the 'famous' people in Hollywood to denounce violence against the President of the United States.

The hatred is so palpable. Bill Maher once compared Trump to an orangutan. What a disgusting and racist thing. Amanda Seyfried said "Didn't think I was capable of feeling hatred like this. The biggest insult to our country is this snorting piece of garbage."[1] Implying that President Trump did cocaine. She also asked, "Why are we still watching a delusional, racist man-child run for dictator?". Will Smith said "For a man to be able to publicly refer to a woman as a fat pig, that makes me teary. And for people to applaud, that is absolutely fucking insanity to me... If one of my sons, I am getting furious just thinking about it, if one of my sons said that in a public place, they couldn't even live in my house anymore... For me, deep down in my heart, I believe that America won't and we can't [elect Donald Trump]. Of all the things he has said, and we could go through the laundry list, that was the one that was such an absolute illustration of a darkness of his soul. I just cannot figure out how people can clap for that." He also said before the election that America had a chance to "cleanse" itself of Trump supporters, saying "As painful as it is to hear Donald Trump talk and as embarrassing as it is as an American to hear him talk, I think it's good," Smith continued: "We get to know who people are and now we get to cleanse it out of our country."[2] Robert De Niro had kind words for our President "He's so blatantly stupid. He's a punk, he's a dog, he's a pig, he's a con — a bullshit artist. A mutt who doesn't know what he's talking about, doesn't do his homework, doesn't care, thinks he's gaming society, doesn't pay his taxes. He's an idiot." The very vicious and nasty Elizabeth Banks: "Let's give it back to him ladies. The Donald is a -4. Fat old orange POS. #giveback." She tweeted. Johnny Depp had an optimistic message: "If Donald Trump is elected president of the United States in a kind of historical way, it's exciting because we will see the actual last president of the United States. It just won't work after that." Depp has also threatened President Trump with assassination since I initially wrote this chapter. Cher tweeted "let's throw Trump in a volcano." Jennifer Lawrence said that "If Donald Trump becomes president, that will be the end of the world."[3] Yeah, that's right, if the working-middle class gets a tax cut, it will be the end of the world. Elitist George Clooney had an insightful message when he said "He's just an opportunist. Now he's a fascist; a xenophobic fascist."[4] Chelsea Handler said "It's kind of great to have a person like that represent everything that's wrong in the world. It's always a good thing to look at somebody and say, 'That's the worst thing that could happen.' I think we should keep [Trump] in the spotlight— not as a president, obviously." Just an endless stream of pure hatred. Many in Hollywood also threatened to go on strike because of President Trump, and I wish they would, maybe we could get a break from their propaganda and bullshit for a few minutes. Of course, many celebrities also threatened to leave the United States altogether including: Bryan Cranston, Miley Cyrus, Supreme Court Justice Ruth Bader Ginsburg, Lena Dunham, Spike Lee, Amber Rose, Amy Schumer, Jon Stewart, Cher, Chelsea Handler, Samuel L. Jackson, Neve Campbell, Keegan-Michael Key, George Lopez, Ne-Yo, Al Sharpton, Raven-Symoné, and Barbra Streisand just to name a few. It's now Summer 2017, and these people still haven't moved out of the Country. I'm waiting. America is waiting. Sean Hannity offered to pay for their flights out of the Country (with the stipulation that it's one way). I think they should take up Hannity's offer and move to another country since they said they would.

The truth is that many of these celebrities are nothing more than puppets. It's the producers, shareholders, and production company owners who have a major stranglehold on power in Hollywood. It's these people who set the radical leftist, globalist, open borders, big government, high taxes, social justice warrior, liberal agenda. These are radical leftist individuals. They want expanded government, globalism, and tyranny. They expect you to want it as well. You either toe the line and play along, or you get demonized, blacklisted, and cast aside. It's extraordinarily difficult to survive as a conservative in Hollywood as we all know, but just how difficult is it really? Well if you happen to have any kind of opinion on anything that differs from the pack, you're just not allowed to talk about that. Have something to say about Obamacare being a disaster? Have something to say about the threats of open borders? Have something to say that is critical of Islam? Have something critical to say about the IRS targeting conservative groups for the crime of existing? Have something critical to say about Obama or Hillary? Have something to say about the national debt? Have something to say about the crumbling infrastructure in America? Have something to say about the out of control welfare state? Have something to say about authoritarian bureaucrats in Washington DC? Have something positive to say about President Trump? Want to say something positive about conservatives, or gun owners, or farmers? Have anything to say at all? Too bad. You're not allowed. You think you have free speech in this Country? Sadly, the discrimination is very real and very agonizing to watch. Not only is the blacklisting alive and well, it's thriving and flourishing, and as Americans, we've become totally numb to it which is even sadder. We'll put up with anything. The conservative actors lose potential jobs, are looked down upon, shunned, demonized, and treated as outcasts. There is no rush of your fellow entertainment industry colleagues running to your side to defend you. You're isolated, attacked, and alone. There are bullying tactics, death threats, smears, racial slurs, and the most vicious language you could possibly imagine, all used against people. Look at what happened to Broadway star Jennifer Holliday, who performed for George W. Bush and Barack Obama, yet she had to cancel her appearance at President Trump's inauguration celebration.[5] Not only was she being bullied and called racial slurs, but she was also receiving death threats as well saying:

> "I've spent all day yesterday and all last night reading all the terrible things that people were saying about me.
> And even being called by my own black people a "n—er," a "house n—er," "c—n, "Uncle Tom," people suggesting I should kill myself, a "traitor," all kinds of things. It was very frightening and very alarming and overwhelming, as well, to see those kinds of things about you. It'd be different if I'm out there all the time trying to make headlines or something."

Many others were blacklisted and threatened to not perform. Some were even viciously attacked for simply not wanting to go along with the delegitimizing campaign against President Trump. Actress Nicole Kidman just wanted less fighting and division in the country. She said, "I just say, [Trump's] now elected, and we as a country need to support whoever's the president because that's what the country's based on."[6] Not only did Kidman get ferocious backlash and hatred from the left, but her career was also threatened. Joss Whedon, the authoritarian man who helped give us "The Avengers", which I could certainly live without, attacked her looks, her intelligence, and credibility all in one tweet. I think the real disgusting individual is Joss Whedon with his bullying and his pure hatred for the first amendment and any speech he disagrees with.

Hypocrisy isn't the right word when it comes to Hollywood. The actors and producers who push their tyranny on the masses are more than just hypocritical. They're insane, delusional, fraudulent, deceptive, self-righteous, artificial, lying, hollow, faithless, insincere, selfish, God hating, freedom hating Hypocrites. They hate America. They're nothing but a giant pile of lies. They claim to care for the poor, but what kind of policies do they promote? They support failed policies that keep people dependent on government. They promote a failed welfare state where people never achieve their real potential, and they never reach the American dream. They love making the US the highest taxed nation on earth, so the middle class can never make any real progress towards upward mobility. They promote the "refugee" program of bringing in terrorists and Islamic militants into America. Will they house these people? Will the terrorist refugees be accommodated in their plethora of mansions with 20 bedrooms and large estates guarded by massive walls and security forces? NO. You get the terrorists brought into your neighborhood, so they can take your jobs, commit crimes against Americans, and support Sharia Law over the Constitution. Just Look at Paris, the "City of Lights" now, after having brought in refugees. Images of Paris filled with garbage, urine, feces, dirty mattresses, crime, disease, chaos, and absolute insanity.

Hollywood also supports disarming you and taking away your ability to defend yourself. They hate the Second Amendment. The entertainment industry has made billions off of action films that have guns in them, but in real life, they want strict gun control. They get armed bodyguards and advanced security details, and you're not even allowed to protect your family. Matt Damon who's made millions off of the 'Bourne' Film Series supports gun control. Liam Neeson from the 'Taken' Franchise which is filled with weapons and action scenes, supports gun control and has criticized the NRA. Hundreds of others do as well. It's also hypocritical of these celebrities to say that they know what's best for America when they can't even read from a card. Last night at the Oscars, which I didn't watch, apparently they announced the wrong film for Best Picture. They were too busy worshipping themselves and their golden calves, idols, and their own selfishness. They were too busy savagely and viciously attacking President Trump to be able to read from a card correctly. Alleged comedian Kathy Griffin held a photoshoot which simulated her holding the decapitated and bloodied head of President Trump. It was literally just like ISIS. It was a terrorist threat. Trump's eleven-year-old son Barron Trump thought it was actually his dad. Kathy Griffin then comes out for a press conference after a public backlash and claims that she's the real victim. Absolute insanity. Johnny Depp has also threatened assassination against our President.

Many in Hollywood are obsessed with thinking they are more powerful than ordinary people. Not just by having more money, living extravagant lifestyles, having mega mansions all over the world, private jets, luxurious travel, etc. but also feeling like they are generally more advanced intellectually and spiritually. Their interest in Scientology is nothing more than a cult following. The same applies to the Illuminati. You can see Illuminati imagery all over the Entertainment industry. Author Mark Dice explains this in his books on the subject which people should check out. Mark Dice also has videos on YouTube which I enjoy, where he points out the ridiculous nature of celebrities in general.

But it's not just that celebrities are delusional and selfish people. Many are also predatory by nature. The history of pedophilia in Hollywood is well known. Producer Roman Polanski pleaded guilty to unlawful sexual intercourse with a minor. He sexually assaulted and raped a 13-year-old girl. Polanski then fled the country and avoided justice. Many still stood up and gave him a standing ovation in the early 2000's. Hollywood literally gave a standing ovation and an award to an admitted pedophile. Absolutely disgusting. That's Hollywood. Jared Fogle, the Subway guy, was found guilty on child pornography charges. Actor Jeffrey Jones, who was a character in 'Beetlejuice,' and played 'Edward Rooney' in 'Ferris Bueller's Day Off' was arrested in 2002 for possession of child pornography and solicitation of a minor, whom he had pose for nude photographs. He is now a registered sex offender. Paul Gadd, known as Gary Glitter, was a singer, songwriter, and musician and is currently incarcerated. He was convicted and sentenced to 16 years in prison in 2015. This slime-ball has a long history of child pornography, sex with underage girls, child abuse, rape, and all kinds of charges all over the world. Then there was Jimmy Savile, who was called Sir Jimmy Savile in England. Savile was an English DJ and television/radio personality. The crimes against Savile are too long to list. The National Society for the Prevention of Cruelty to Children (NSPCC) had a report saying 450 people made complaints/charges against Savile. The period of child abuse went on from 1955 to 2009. The suspected victims' list includes 28 children under the age of 10 and 63 girls between the ages of 13 and 16. Dozens of rapes were recorded spanning dozens of police forces. Jimmy Savile died in 2011, and he's not having fun anymore.

Here are a few Quotes which illustrate how bad Hollywood is.[7]

"Hollywood is a place where they'll pay you a thousand dollars for a kiss and fifty cents for your soul."

—Marilyn Monroe

"Hollywood is run by people who sit up in their executive office, who are not connected to Mississippi, Alabama, Chicago, South Carolina. They know nothing about that, they don't go to church, and they make their decisions about what they think is right."

—Steve Harvey

"I love Los Angeles, and I love Hollywood. They're beautiful. Everybody's plastic, but I love plastic. I want to be plastic."

—Andy Warhol

The point is that Hollywood fundamentally despises the hardworking middle-class conservatives in this country. They look down and hate working folks. They dislike God. They don't like Freedom. They loathe the Constitution. They detest fly-over country. They abhor any small semblance remaining of traditional values in America. They don't just hate President Trump. They also hate the people he represents. Hollywood is satanic to its core. So, what can we do? We can peacefully boycott them. Stop supporting Hollywood. Stop supporting their movies. Stop supporting these actors who despise freedom and want tyranny. We don't owe anything to Hollywood. Send them a message, peacefully, that we're sick of their garbage and bullying and hatred. Instead of going to the movies, do something else instead. Plant a garden. Go outside and exercise. Read some books. Go for a bike ride. Go hiking. Help some homeless people. Do something charitable with your close friends and family. Go exercise or play some sports with friends. Visit a museum. Enjoy nature. Go golfing. Support President Trump. Help Make America Great Again. Do something positive with your time rather than support Hollywood.

Nine

UNITED NATIONS

When was the United Nations created? What was its original purpose? What is its history? What are the components that make up the United Nations? How is it funded? Why does the United States have to carry such a heavy burden in the funding? Why has the UN failed to prevent conflicts? Why is it so ineffective and inefficient? Why is there so much bureaucratic waste and abuse in the UN? What kinds of corruption have affected the United Nations? Why does the UN so desperately want to shut down American energy? What was the UN's connection to Obama's nightmare Iran deal? Why is the UN so anti-Israel?

The United Nations is one of the main components of globalism in the world. It's supported by many of America's enemies and supports policies that hurt the US. The United Nations supports collectivism and promotes a concentration of power in the hands of select global elites. It costs us billions every year and creates policies averse to our own interests. In this chapter, I'll make the case as to why the US should either leave the United Nations or at the very least dramatically reduce our funding to it even more.

The United Nations was formed in 1945 after World War II, and its purpose was to prevent more wars. The world was tired of war and carnage. The Allied Powers had big plans and wanted to work cooperatively in the effort to create a new entity which could help stop more deadly conflicts. The United Nations Charter was drafted. There was a UN Conference on International Organization in San Francisco in April 1945.[1] The convention had delegates from many Allied Nations. It wasn't until October of that year that the United Nations officially started as an entity. The Charter had to first be ratified by the five large powers: The US, UK, France, Soviet Union, and the Republic of China. The first meetings of the General Assembly happened in London after that. New York City was eventually picked as the chosen location for the United Nations headquarters, and the complex was finished in 1952 in Manhattan. The Rockefellers wanted the United Nations headquartered on their estate in Kykuit (Rockefeller Estate in Westchester County, NY) but it was considered too far from Manhattan. So instead, the Rockefellers bought land from a real estate developer and then "donated" it. The Rockefellers then had their personal architect (who was also a brother-in-law to a Rockefeller daughter) become the director of planning of the UN compound, as his firm would monitor the implementation of the design. This area is considered extraterritorial, meaning it's just its own international territory, separate from the US government. Additionally, there are three more regional headquarters in Geneva, Switzerland; Vienna, Austria; and Nairobi, Kenya.

The United Nations has five main components. They include the International Court of Justice, the Secretariat, the Economic and Social Council, the Security Council, and the General Assembly. The International Court of Justice deals with legal disputes and gives judgments by a relative majority. It is composed of fifteen judges, who are each elected to nine-year terms. The judges are elected by the UN General Assembly and the UN Security Council, and they come from a list of nominees provided by the Permanent Court of Arbitration. There is a rule which states that no two judges can be nationals of the same country. The Secretariat is the executive branch of the United Nations. It helps set the agenda for the entire United Nations. The Secretary General is the top person of the Secretariat and is responsible for settling international disputes, peacekeeping operations, conducting international conferences, and helping the Security Council. The Economic and Social Council has 54 members from all over the world. The council works with the specialized agencies throughout the UN and helps them organize the economic and social work. The Security Council's job is to preserve international peace and safety. The Security Council also has the task of accepting new members to the United Nations. There are only fifteen members of the security council, and they have immense power including the use of international sanctions, authorization of military force through Security Council resolutions, and they approve any changes to the UN Charter. Finally, there is the General Assembly. This is where all member countries have equal representation. The General Assembly helps make the UN operate. It oversees the budget, appoints certain members of the Security Council, all the members of the Economic and Social Council, the fifteen judges of the International Court of Justice, and the UN Secretary General.

The United Nations has failed to prevent many conflicts and deaths over the decades. This includes the genocide that happened in Rwanda in the early 1990's.

In 1994, it was estimated that over 800,000 people were killed in Rwanda, specifically hitting the Tutsi population. The Genocide took place during a 100-day hellish death spree spanning from April to

July. There were also many tens of thousands of rapes and an increase in HIV-infected people. Babies were killed in the genocide and others were born to HIV-infected mothers as a result of rape. Bloodthirsty militias were fierce, vicious, and merciless towards their victims. Church altars became areas of execution. People were hacked to death with machetes, stabbed with spears/knives, and killed in the most brutal ways imaginable. There were so many dead bodies scattered over the countryside that bulldozers were used to gather their remains. It was absolute hell on earth, and the United Nations failed miserably. The UN also failed to prevent the Cambodian genocide that took place in the 1970's. Millions of Cambodians died between the years 1975-1979. The Khmer Rouge, KR regime was led by Pol Pot, and they were responsible for the genocide. There was torture, mass executions, starvation, and disease. People were forced to relocate. Roughly a quarter of the country's population died. Tens of thousands of mass graves have been found. This was a real atrocity and a real nightmare. It was horrific beyond words. Yet some very selfish and ignorant people in America compare the 2016 presidential election and the victory of President Donald J Trump to some kind of atrocity of this nature. What a disgrace. The UN has also failed to prevent the Vietnam War, the war in Iraq, and many other civil wars around the globe.

The United Nations gets funding from many countries, obviously. But what percentage of the UN's annual budget does each country contribute? We give by far the most, and it's not even a contest. The United States of America provides 22% of the United Nations annual budget (2016). Japan is second; they give the UN 9.68% of its budget. The third is China (7.921%). Germany is fourth, contributing 6.389%. France is fifth at 4.859%.

Many others give tiny amounts. Some of these countries are incredibly wealthy, and they're ripping us off "Big League" to quote our President. There's no debate about that. Canada doesn't even give 3%.

Australia is a wealthy nation, and they only give 2.337%. Mexico is at 1.435%, what a disgrace. Our enemy, Saudi Arabia (Remember that 15 of the 19, September 11th hijackers were citizens of Saudi Arabia) gives 1.146% of the UN Budget. Saudi Arabia is a very wealthy country rich with oil. They need to share more of the cost. Switzerland contributes 1.14% of the UN's budget. Why should we pay the majority of it when a lot of these countries hate America? Sounds fair. Also, there's the fact that the UN is incredibly wasteful with its funds. There is massive incompetence, waste, fraud, and abuse that goes on. So much of the UN's money is lost through its inefficient and ineffective agencies.

There is also massive amounts of corruption that goes on all the time at the United Nations.[2] U.S. authorities even brought charges against a bunch of people related to UN corruption and bribery schemes.[3]

Anthony Banbury was an Assistant Secretary General for Field Support for the United Nations. He resigned on February 5, 2016, because of a lack of accountability, saying that the UN was in need of "reform." Banbury then wrote for the NY times, explaining some of the problems that go on at the United Nations.[4] The column was entitled "I Love the U.N., but It Is Failing". Here are a few quotes from Banbury's column:

> "Six years ago, I became an assistant secretary general, posted to the headquarters in New York. I was no stranger to red tape, but I was unprepared for the blur of Orwellian admonitions and Carrollian logic that govern the place. If you locked a team of evil geniuses in a laboratory, they could not design a bureaucracy so maddeningly complex, requiring so much effort but in the end incapable of delivering the intended result. The system is a black hole into which disappear countless tax dollars and human aspirations, never to be seen again."

"The heads of billion-dollar peace operations, with enormous responsibilities for ending wars, are not able to hire their immediate staff, or to reassign non-performers away from critical roles. It is a sign of how perversely twisted the bureaucracy is that personnel decisions are considered more dangerous than the responsibility to lead a mission on which the fate of a country depends."

"One result of this dysfunction is minimal accountability. There is today a chief of staff in a large peacekeeping mission who is manifestly incompetent. Many have tried to get rid of him, but short of a serious crime, it is virtually impossible to fire someone in the United Nations. In the past six years, I am not aware of a single international field staff member's being fired, or even sanctioned, for poor performance."

"In early 2013, the United Nations decided to send 10,000 soldiers and police officers to Mali in response to a terrorist takeover... Inexplicably, we sent a force that was unprepared for counterterrorism and explicitly told not to engage in it. More than 80 percent of the force's resources are spent on logistics and self-protection."

"BUT the thing that has upset me most is what the United Nations has done in the Central African Republic. When we took over peacekeeping responsibilities from the African Union there in 2014, we had the choice of which troops to accept. Without appropriate debate, and for cynical political reasons, a decision was made to include soldiers from the Democratic Republic of Congo and from the Republic of Congo, despite reports of serious human rights violations by these soldiers. Since then, troops from these countries have engaged in a persistent pattern of rape and abuse of the people — often young girls — the United Nations was sent there to protect."

"Last year, peacekeepers from the Republic of Congo arrested a group of civilians, with no legal basis whatsoever, and beat them so badly that one died in custody and the other shortly after in a hospital. In response there was hardly a murmur, and certainly no outrage, from the responsible officials in New York."

"...my first job with the United Nations was as a human rights officer in Cambodian refugee camps along the Thai-Cambodian border, investigating rapes and murders of the poor and helpless. Never could I have imagined that I would one day have to deal with members of my own organization committing the same crimes or, worse, senior officials tolerating them for reasons of cynical expediency."

The United Nations spends tens of billions of dollars every year, and a lot of that money magically goes missing. The UN, by its own admission, admits how challenging and arduous it is for them as an organization to deal with the fraud and theft that goes on there. A select group of experts carried out examinations throughout UN funds, programs, and various organizations.[5] In a document entitled "FRAUD PREVENTION, DETECTION AND RESPONSE IN UNITED NATIONS SYSTEM ORGANIZATIONS" released in 2016, by members of the world organization's Joint Inspection Unit (JIU) it discusses these challenges:

"B. Challenges of pursuing perpetrators

301. In most organizations interviewed, there were various incidents where the subject of allegation would resign and/or move to another organization prior to or during the investigation or disciplinary process. The Inspectors were informed that in most such cases disciplinary measures were not subsequently imposed against the individuals concerned, as

the organization does not have the authority to enforce such measures on former staff members. In some organizations, a note may be placed in the personnel file of the former staff member indicating he/she was subject to an investigation or disciplinary process and that the case was not concluded.

302. Investigating units in a number of organizations reported that they have the discretion to continue investigations into possible misuses of human and financial resources, whether or not the subject is current or former personnel. However, once a staff member has resigned, he/she is no longer under the authority of the organization. As such, he/she could no longer be compelled to cooperate with an investigation that may be ongoing. Indeed, the United Nations Dispute Tribunal, in a ruling of 2010 on this issue, has held that an exstaff member "cannot be compelled to be involved, let alone cooperate". This could significantly impede the investigation, as it makes the collection and analysis of evidence much more difficult or even impossible. It was observed that other multinational entities have provisions in place ensuring former staff members' obligation to cooperate with the organizations in respect of investigations. Such provisions help to prevent staff members under investigation impeding the conduct of investigations by unilaterally disengaging from the organization.

303. **It is recommended that the executive heads of the United Nations system organizations instruct their respective legal offices to review the approach to cases where the subject of investigations resigns unilaterally, so as to ensure continuation of the investigations, as warranted, including the obligation of the subject to cooperate with the investigators, as well as recovery of damages, including**

from the staff members' pension, as appropriate (the reader should also refer to paragraphs 306 to 327 below on referrals).

304. It was also disclosed during interviews that, owing to legal and confidentiality concerns, information on a staff member who is under investigation or has been disciplined, are not shared with other United Nations system organizations at the time of recruitment of this individual by another United Nations system organization. Some organizations are considering including questions in their job application forms requesting the applicant, in addition to the commonly used questions on previous criminal indictments, to provide information on possible investigation and disciplinary history with other employers along the lines "Have you been the subject of an investigation and/or disciplinary process of another employer, including by a United Nations system or international organization? If so, please explain." The specific language is still under consideration in these organizations by legal and human resources offices.

305. **It is recommended that United Nations system organizations include in application forms specific questions on staff's previous involvement in fraudulent activities and the outcome of such activities and/or investigations. Any possible legal issues related to such action should be reviewed and cleared in advance by the legal office. Furthermore, the legal and human resources networks of HLCM should consult on a common approach and language to address this matter.**

Referral of cases to national judicial and enforcement authorities

306. In strengthening the disciplinary measures imposed by the United Nations system organizations, but also in view

of the challenges in pursuing action against former staff members, referral of cases to national authorities, in particular for criminal and civil proceedings and/or for recovery of fraud losses, gain additional importance.

307. The United Nations cooperates with law enforcement and the judicial authorities of relevant Member States in accordance with its rights and obligations under the Convention on the Privileges and Immunities of the United Nations, adopted by the General Assembly on 13 February 1946, as well as other relevant international agreements and applicable legal principles.

308. Section 21 of the Convention on the Privileges and Immunities of the United Nations ("the General Convention") stipulates that the United Nations should cooperate at all times with the appropriate authorities of Members to facilitate the proper administration of justice, secure the observance of regulations and prevent the occurrence of any abuse in connection with the privileges, immunities and facilities mentioned in article V of the General Convention. Moreover, in accordance with the Staff Regulations and Rules of the United Nations, officials and experts on mission, are required to comply with local laws and honour their private legal obligations.156

309. It is the policy of the United Nations that officials and experts on mission should be held accountable whenever they commit criminal acts, including fraud and corruption, not only because of the harm caused to the victims but also because they undermine the work and image of the United Nations. Consequently, where the United Nations, after proper internal investigation using its own investigative processes, establishes credible allegations that reveal that a crime may have been committed by United Nations officials

or experts on mission, such allegations when proven credible are ordinarily brought to the attention of/referred to the Member State having jurisdiction over the alleged conduct. Given the legal issues involved in the referral to the relevant State, and the implication on the privileges and immunities of the United Nations, all such cases are reviewed by the OLA before a final determination is made on referring the case to authorities. OLA consults with the relevant programme managers, as appropriate, to determine the wider interests of the United Nations in pursuing a particular case. OLA conducts referrals concerning all departments of the United Nations Secretariat, as well as all the funds and programmes of the United Nations."

A UN audit showed serious problems which linked to more possible bribery.[6] But it's not just that the UN is inefficient, ineffective, and corrupt. It has a history that more people need to understand. In 1992 the United Nations had an environmental conference in Brazil. They created an action plan called "Agenda 21, " and it was later published in 1993. It was about "sustainability" issues on the planet in regards to both the climate and population.[7] Here is one paragraph from the large document:

"Basis for action

5.42. Population programmes are more effective when implemented together with appropriate crosssectoral policies. To attain sustainability at the local level, a new framework is needed that integrates demographic trends and factors with such factors as ecosystem health, technology and human settlements, and with socio-economic structures and access to resources. Population programmes should be consistent with socio-economic and environmental planning. Integrated sustainable development programmes should closely correlate action on demographic trends and factors with resource management activities and development goals that meet the needs of the people concerned."

The Republican party rightfully opposed the Agenda 21 and said: "We strongly reject the U.N. Agenda 21 as erosive of American sovereignty." The United Nations wants us to follow stringent environmental policies that would hurt our coal miners and would shut down our energy production. Energy costs would continue to go through the roof if it were up to the UN. Meanwhile, China, as we discussed earlier, has no environmental standards of any kind. The UN was also very supportive of the catastrophic 'Iran deal.' They really wanted that deal and voted in favor of it. A deal that was bad for America and bad for Israel. A deal that gave Iran $150 Billion dollars. People living on planet Earth know that Iran supports and funds all kinds of terrorism. They chant "death to America" and "death to Israel." They call the United States the "Great Satan" and Israel "Little Satan." They hate us, want us dead, and yet the United Nations votes in favor of this disgraceful deal. The UN also wants us to take in Islamic militants that they call "refugees." We discussed what happened to Paris after "refugees" came there. Europe is a mess. That's what the UN thinks of the United States. We're their number one financial contributor, and they want us to be filled with Islamic militants and terrorists causing death, violence, disease, chaos, and fear. The United Nations is an absolute disgrace, and it has made the world more chaotic and more destabilized. It has jeopardized our security and well-being, as well as Israel's, and is actively working against our own interests. Why should we be the number one contributor to a group that is working against us? Seems like a fair question to me. We need to have a serious debate in America about the United Nations, and we should either leave it entirely or at the very least continue to reduce our funding even more.

Ten

ACADEMIA

W e have a situation that is completely out of control. Our institutions of higher education and learning have totally rotted from the inside. American colleges and universities have so many problems that it's strenuous to know exactly where to begin. There's a sickness and a disease that infests our places of higher learning. It's cancer that is very dangerous. There was always a liberal bias in these institutions, but it's now so lopsided and biased, it's absurd.

In this chapter, we will discuss Academia. We'll discuss the extreme biases, and just how radical and disturbed some of these professors are. We'll explain the history of Cloward and Piven at Columbia University and their dangerous ideas. We'll examine the political agenda being pushed at Colleges and Universities today such as wealth redistribution, environmental extremism, open borders, sanctuary campuses for illegal aliens, and support for radical Islamic terrorism and groups like black lives matter. I'll investigate how huge the problem of student loan debt is, and why so many people are getting conned. Next, we'll talk about the bullying of conservatives that goes on, including violence, censorship, and harassment. Finally, we'll discuss the overwhelming elitism, arrogance, smugness, and politically correct attitude that is so pervasive in these universities, specifically their administrators.

In October of 2016, there was a poll released by the William F. Buckley, Jr. Program at Yale. The poll found that 80%, or 4 out of every five college students said their professors "generally prefer" Hillary Clinton for President of the States. The few professors in America who support Trump are faced with a vicious backlash. A backlash that comes not only from liberal students, but also from fellow professors who disagree with them politically, the college board itself, often the dean of the school, and even liberal alumni associations. You will feel alone, isolated, silenced, and like you're in a hostile environment. That's because you are. It's is very difficult for conservative professors who support Trump. College and Universities' faculty members also contributed to Hillary through financial donations at a staggering level. A story at 'thecrimson.com' by Melissa C. Rodman and Luca F. Schroeder entitled *"Faculty Overwhelmingly Donate to Clinton"* had data analysis by Idrees M. Kahloon and Luca F. Schroeder. The story explained how 91% of political contributions by Harvard staff went to Hillary.[1] Here is a short excerpt from the story:

"Ninety-one percent of contributions to current presidential candidates made by Harvard faculty, instructors, and researchers in 2015 went to former Secretary of State Hillary R. Clinton, according to a Crimson analysis of Federal Election Commission filings.

Between April and December of 2015, a total of 81 Harvard faculty, instructors, and researchers donated roughly $131,000 to the presidential campaigns of Clinton, Vermont Senator Bernie Sanders, former Florida Governor Jeb Bush, Florida Senator Marco Rubio, and New Jersey Governor Chris Christie.

Of the individuals who donated, 37 gave the maximum contribution for the primary period—$2,700—to Clinton."

This was the case everywhere. All of these places wanted Hillary.[2] She dominated Harvard, Yale, UC Berkeley, Columbia, Stanford, Dartmouth, University of Chicago, Duke, and New York University just to name a few. Some of their professors' events went so far as to send their students liberal messaging directly. An article on thegatewaypundit.com titled *"Professor Spams His Students to Support Crooked Hillary, Then Blames It On Hackers"* explained a situation like this. An arrogant leftist professor, Billy Riggs, who teaches urban policy economics spammed his students to support Hillary.[3] Here is a section from the article:

> "A professor at California State Polytechnic Institute appears to have lied about his email being hacked after sending a message to his students asking them to vote for Hillary Clinton.
>
> Billy Riggs, an assistant professor of City & Regional Planning at Cal Poly, sent an email to his entire department Sunday pledging his support for Hillary Clinton and asking students and colleagues to do the same. The email was sent through "Brigade," a mobile app that matches users to candidates based on how they respond to political questions.
>
> 'Billy has pledged to vote for Hillary Clinton on Brigade, the world's first voter network. Join them and pledge your vote, learn about issues, and take positions. Billy wants you to pledge to vote for Hillary Clinton,' the email read."

Some professors told their students that the Earth would fry if they didn't support Hillary. Yet President Trump was the one who got accused of using fear tactics. The ones using fear tactics were these climate alarmist professors telling their students the world would literally end if they didn't vote for Hillary. In fact, hundreds of members of the US National Academy of Sciences signed an open letter before the election which supported Hillary because of 'global warming'. They were all in. They were '#withher' and thought it was a done deal. It was supposed to be all wrapped up. It was a sure thing. Imagine the surprise and shock that Academia went through when President Trump won. In fact, it was more than the shock that they experienced. They literally needed coloring books to cope with the election loss. What a bunch of babies. There are hard-working Americans who do incredibly tough work every day and have physical pain from it. When the government raised their taxes, over regulated them, wrecked their economy, let their roads/bridges/highways/tunnels fall apart, raised their healthcare costs, raised their energy costs, and shipped their jobs overseas…they didn't need coloring books, crayons, play dough, Lego bricks, bubbles, puppies, hot chocolate, and 'cry ins' to mourn. That was the snot-nosed, selfish, entitled, authoritarian students and faculty at elite campuses around America who needed those things. Also, 'President Trump Stress Disorder' is not a real thing. He wants to Make America Great Again, cut your taxes, rebuild the country, grow the economy, get rid of the debt, bring unity to the country, keep the country safe, and bring back the American spirit and the American dream. Claiming 'President Trump Stress Disorder' is a disgrace which brings dishonor, disrespect, and shame to our real heroes, our Brave Veterans. Imagine you're a veteran who risked your life for America and our freedoms, had friends killed in combat, and went through absolute hell, many losing arms or legs in different conflicts. Those heroes are the ones who sometimes deal with real Post Traumatic Stress Disorder from the sacrifices they went through. Their courage, honor, strength, and dedication to America is something these elitists in the academic world should learn about.

Of Course, this type of insanity is nothing new in Academia, sadly. Just look at Cloward and Piven for example. Richard Cloward and Frances Fox Piven were a husband-wife professor team at Columbia University. They were married and both professors at the Columbia University School of Social Work. They developed a strategy known as the Cloward-Piven strategy. They believed in a guaranteed annual income to combat poverty. Their strategy was to overload the US welfare system with so many recipients that it would cause a crisis, in their own words. Their hopes were that this manufactured crisis would lead to the political reforms that they desired. If they wanted to combat poverty, they should have promoted free market values and using hard work to achieve the American dream, not by helping exacerbate a welfare problem and causing a crisis to achieve their goals. Their strategy was explained in 1966 in 'The Nation', a liberal magazine. The article was called *"The Weight of the Poor: A Strategy to End Poverty"* by Frances Fox Piven and Richard Cloward.[4] Here are some quotes from their article:

"How can the poor be organized to press for relief from poverty? How can a broad-based movement be developed and the current disarray of activist forces be halted? These questions confront, and confound, activists today. It is our purpose to advance a strategy which affords the basis for a convergence of civil rights organizations, militant anti-poverty groups and the poor. If this strategy were implemented, **a political crisis would result** that could lead to legislation for a guaranteed annual income and thus an end to poverty. The strategy is based on the fact that a vast discrepancy exists between the benefits to which people are entitled under public welfare programs and the sums which they actually receive. This gulf is not recognized in a society that is wholly and self-righteously oriented toward getting people *off* the welfare rolls. It is widely known, for example, that nearly 8 million persons (half of them white) now subsist on welfare, but it is not generally known that for every person on the rolls at least one more probably meets existing criteria of eligibility but is not obtaining assistance.

The discrepancy is not an accident stemming from bureaucratic inefficiency; rather, it is an integral feature of the welfare system, which, if challenged, **would precipitate a profound financial and political crisis**. The force for that challenge, and the strategy we propose, is a massive drive to recruit the poor *onto* the welfare rolls. The distribution of public assistance has been a local and state responsibility, and that accounts in large part for the abysmal character of welfare practices. Despite the growing involvement of federal agencies in supervisory and reimbursement arrangements, state and local community forces are still decisive. The poor are most visible and proximate in the local community; antagonism toward them (and toward the agencies which are implicated with them) has always, therefore, been more intense locally than at the federal level. In recent years, local communities have increasingly felt class and ethnic friction generated by competition for neighborhoods, schools, jobs and political power. Public welfare systems are under the constant stress of conflict and opposition, made only sharper by the rising costs to localities of public aid. And, to accommodate this pressure, welfare practice everywhere has become more restrictive than welfare statute; much of the time it verges on lawlessness. Thus, public welfare systems try to keep their budgets down and their rolls low by failing to inform people of the rights available to them; by intimidating and shaming them to the degree that they are reluctant either to apply or to press claims, and by arbitrarily denying benefits to those who are eligible. A series of welfare drives in large cities would, we believe, impel action on a new federal program to distribute income, eliminating the present public welfare system and alleviating the abject poverty which it perpetrates. Widespread campaigns to register the eligible poor for welfare aid, and to help existing recipients obtain their full benefits, would produce bureaucratic disruption in welfare agencies and fiscal disruption in local and state governments. These disruptions would generate severe political strains, and deepen existing divisions among elements in the big-city Democratic coalition: the remaining white middle class, the white working-class ethnic groups and the growing minority poor. To avoid a further weakening of that historic coalition, a national Democratic administration would be constrained to advance a federal solution to poverty that would override local welfare failures, local class and racial conflicts and local revenue dilemmas. By the internal disruption of local bureaucratic practices, by the furor over public welfare poverty, and by the collapse of current financing arrangements, powerful forces can be generated for major economic reforms at the national level."

"Because the ideal of individual social and economic mobility has deep roots, even activists seem reluctant to call for national programs to eliminate poverty by the outright redistribution of income."

"But many of the contemporary poor will not rise from poverty by organizing to bargain collectively. They either are not in the labor force or are in such marginal and dispersed occupations (e.g., domestic servants) that it is extremely difficult to organize them. Compared with other groups, then, many of today's poor cannot secure a redistribution of income by organizing within the institution of private enterprise. A federal program of income redistribution has become necessary to elevate the poor en masse from poverty."

"**In order to generate a crisis**, the poor must obtain benefits, which they have forfeited. Until now, they have been inhibited from asserting claims by self-protective devices within the welfare system: its capacity to limit information, to intimidate applicants, to demoralize recipients, and arbitrarily to deny lawful claims.

Ignorance of welfare rights can be attacked through a massive educational campaign Brochures describing benefits in simple, clear language, and urging people to seek their full entitlements, should be distributed door to door in tenements and public housing projects, and deposited in stores, schools, churches and civic centers. Advertisements should be placed in newspapers; sport announcements should be made on radio. Leaders of social, religious, fraternal and political groups in the slums should also be enlisted to recruit the eligible to the rolls. The fact that the campaign is intended to inform people of their legal rights under a government program, that it is a civic education drive, will lend it legitimacy.

But information alone will not suffice. Organizers will have to become advocates in order to deal effectively with improper rejections and terminations. The advocate's task is to appraise the circumstances of each case, to argue its merits before welfare, to threaten legal action if satisfaction is not given. In some cases, it will be necessary to contest decisions by requesting a "fair before the appropriate hearing" before the appropriate state supervisory agency; it may occasionally be necessary to use for redress in the courts. Hearings and court actions will require lawyers, many of whom, in cities like New York, can be recruited on a voluntary basis, especially under the banner of a movement to end poverty by a strategy of asserting legal rights. However, most cases will not require an expert knowledge of law, but only of welfare regulations; the rules can be learned by laymen, including welfare recipients themselves (who can help to man "information and advocacy" centers). To aid workers in these centers, handbooks should be prepared describing welfare rights and the tactics to employ in claiming them.

Advocacy must be supplemented by organized demonstrations to create a climate of militancy that will overcome the invidious and immobilizing attitudes which many potential recipients hold toward being "on welfare." In such a (climate, many more poor people are likely to become their own advocates and will not need to rely on aid from organizers.

As the crisis develops, it will be important to use the mass media to inform the broader liberal community about the inefficiencies and injustices of welfare. For example, the system will not be able to process many new applicants because of cumbersome and often unconstitutional investigatory procedures (which cost 20c for every dollar disbursed). As delays mount, so should the public demand that a simplified affidavit supplant these procedures, so that the poor may certify to their condition. If the system reacts by making the proof of eligibility more difficult, the demand should be made that the Department of Health, Education and Welfare dispatch "eligibility registrars" to enforce federal statutes governing local programs. And throughout the crisis, the mass media should be used to advance arguments for a new federal income distribution program."

"The ultimate aim of this strategy is a new program for **direct income distribution**. What reason is there to expect that the federal government will enact such legislation in response to a crisis in the welfare system? We ordinarily think of major legislation as taking form only through established electoral processes. We tend to overlook the force of crisis in precipitating legislative reform, partly because we lack a theoretical framework by which to understand the impact of major disruptions."

"A welfare crisis would, of course, produce dramatic local political crisis, disrupting and exposing rifts among urban groups. Conservative Republicans are always ready to declaim the evils of public welfare, and they would probably be the first to raise a hue and cry. But deeper and politically more telling conflicts would take place within the Democratic coalition. Whites–both working-class ethnic groups and many in the middle class–would be aroused against the ghetto poor, while liberal groups, which until recently have been comforted by the notion that the poor are few and, in any event, receiving the beneficent assistance of public welfare would probably support the movement. Group conflict, spelling political crisis for the local party apparatus, would thus become acute as welfare rolls mounted and the strains on local budgets became more severe. In New York City, where the Mayor is now facing desperate revenue shortages, welfare expenditures are already second only to those for public education."

Naturally, many liberals still think that Cloward and Piven were heroes. They weren't. They wanted to create a crisis. Columbia University should be ashamed. Columbia University is also where Barack Obama went to school (We'll get to Obama's failures and his disgraceful, horrendous, disgusting, hateful legacy in a later chapter). Sadly, this type of political desire for wealth redistribution is still very much alive, and it needs to be called out! When Academia is advocating wealth redistribution, they are advocating theft. Is there massive wealth inequality and income inequality and suffering people today? Yes, absolutely there is. But the Answer is NOT wealth redistribution. The answer is to have REAL free markets and actual real capitalism, not crony capitalism. The answer is real competition and a real free market which will compete with existing monopolies that dominate their specific markets. Competition is a natural and healthy thing which drives up wages, produces better quality services/products, lowers costs, creates innovation, promotes growth, makes us more goal oriented, and makes life better/more exciting.

Earlier we discussed how radical the climate agenda is that Academia pushes forward. They are environmental extremists. Many want all fossil fuel companies shut down entirely through force of government. It would be an energy plan that has extremely high energy costs and if you question that you will be attacked. Try using facts, logic, reason, or data to refute any climate narratives. Good luck. It's well known that many climate scientists have gotten caught adjusting different parameters, scales, and graphs so that they can come to their already favored opinion and predetermined outcome. There is enormous money for grants, research, etc. This obvious conflict of interest needs to be more vigorously and directly pointed out.

Many in the academic world also promote open borders as we know. They would literally just allow anyone to come here. Thank God we have a President who is now working to secure our borders.

These colleges and universities should be publicly shamed for their open border stance. That is the policy that gets people hurt and killed and is unacceptable. I think it's an excellent idea that President Trump opened a new office called VOICE (Victims of Immigration Crime Engagement). What happens with the policy that academia wants? You get two MS-13 gang members in our country illegally, kidnapping and raping a 14-year-old girl and murdering another. They also participated in satanic rituals during the attacks. One of the scumbags, Alvarez-Flores aka "Diabolical" had the inside of his apartment turned into a shrine which was dedicated to their satanic beliefs. They also tattooed one of the victim's legs with an image of the grim reaper. There was also a satanic statue in the apartment. These animals got upset when one of the victims didn't like their satanic rituals. This was absolute torture. The next day, a victim's body was found on the side of a road in Houston. We should pray for these poor victims and their families. As for the two MS-13 gang members, both 18 years old, they waved and smiled during their court appearance when the charges were read against them. What disgusting trash, who should have never been in this country. This is what happens with academia's open border, so we have an obligation to call these people out.

Many of the universities also say they want to be "Sanctuary Campuses." They want to give shelter to illegal aliens.[5] They also call Islam the religion of peace, when it is literally at war with America and wants our utter destruction. Remember the Ohio State terrorist attack in November 2016? The terrorist claimed to be a Somali "refugee." He obviously was NOT. He was an Islamic militant. Abdul Razak Ali Artan was directly inspired by the Islamic State, which caused him to use a Honda Civic as a weapon to hit people before eventually getting out of the car. When he got out, he let out a war cry, while holding a butcher knife. The terrorist was shot and killed, and 13 people were hospitalized for injuries. Academia also supports the domestic terrorist group Black Lives Matter which cowardly calls for attacks against our law enforcement officers.

Not only do conservative students have to listen to this dangerous and vile propaganda. They also amass enormous student loan debt in the process.[6] The total student loan debt in America is well over a trillion dollars. It's a colossal nightmare. I'm not advocating for free tuition like Bernie Sanders, but clearly, these colleges are overcharging for tuition. They need to do things to cut costs and have a better-quality product (education), not charge more and more for a horrible product. That's just common sense. Some people owe more than $100,000 in student loans. Insanity. Right now, many universities are making tons of money while conning their students into paying vast sums to them through loans, for a liberal-propagandized "education." Disgusting.

Conservative students also pay this money so that they can get bullied and harassed for expressing their own beliefs and exercising their first amendment rights. Conservative students are mistreated, graded more harshly, physically attacked, demonized, isolated, censored, and ignored while they are made to feel inferior. Free speech thinkers/supporters are also blocked from going to campuses that are supposed to be beacons of freedom of expression. UC Berkeley was literally at the at the center of the Free Speech movement in the 1960's. Today, Berkeley is not only opposed to free speech, but they are willing to go to extraordinary lengths to shut it down. A Milo Yiannopoulos event was violently shut down, innocent people were attacked, the property was destroyed, death threats were made, and thugs in masks rampaged around.[7] It was chaos and a sad sight to watch. The pure hatred for free speech. I don't want to be North Korea. We shouldn't need swat teams and National Guard to come in just to have pro-free-speech events, yet here we are. The so-called "tolerant" left can't even handle

Yiannopoulos, a flamboyant, gay, Jewish, immigrant from Europe who supports President Trump. This type of censorship, harassment, violence, and Nazi-style tactics that are being used to attack the First Amendment to the Constitution of the United States of America must fail. In order for those attacks to fail it's up to us to peacefully stand up for free speech.

John F. Kennedy said that "The goal of education is the advancement of knowledge and the dissemination of truth." Today, the truth is seen as a bad thing. That must end. We must get to a point in America, where we have real education. Just like Martin Luther King, Jr said "The function of education is to teach one to think intensively and to think critically. Intelligence plus character - that is the goal of true education.". We have an obligation to think critically, read history, be informed, and to speak the truth. We should also be more humble in America. I'm sick to death of the arrogance and elitism of these college administrators and professors who think they're better than everyone, especially middle America. They believe that they are better or more 'enlightened' than the working-class, and that is just not true. Their politically correct, smug attitudes are anti-American. It's time for Academia to start respecting the people who do all the real physical work in our country.

Eleven

Venezuela

L et me write a few sentences that people living on planet earth will understand. Socialism is evil. Socialism is dangerous. Socialism is pure evil. Socialism is a sickness. Over the span of the 2016 Presidential election, many on the left supported Bernie Sanders. This inclination to support socialism needs to be discussed. This attitude of supporting socialism, but acting like it's not socialism is really a form of mental illness. Some may ask, who cares? Bernie Sanders lost so what does it matter. He lost to Hillary in an open and publicly rigged Democrat primary election so why is this relevant. It's relevant because so many millions of brain-washed individuals in America and around the world truly believe in socialism and its failed principles. I'm sick of millennials who initially supported someone like Bernie Sanders when they could have supported President Trump from spring of 2015 like me. I even wanted Donald Trump to run for President in 2012, and I've followed his CPAC speeches and events in the years leading up to 2015 and 2016. That's not because I'm so smart, I'm just aware of reality and what's going on.

It's truly sad to watch young people and even people of all ages firmly believe that socialism will create this type of utopia. I, too, want access to great health care in life. I want people to have access to a real, quality, actual education where people truly learn about history, real life, develop their character and toughness, become better people (caring for others, sympathy, having a heart), learn to question things including themselves, and question the government. I want access to all of these things in America. The key word being access. If I chose, as an individual to get a service or product, whether it's health care, education or whatever, I don't want the government to give it to me for free. I want to pay for it myself, through a free market with real competition, choice, and quality. It's really not complicated. This idea of having the government pay for everything when we're over twenty trillion dollars in debt, not counting the debt associated with crumbling infrastructure, bloated entitlement programs, and too much government regulations.....is madness, dementia, lunacy, and pure idiocy. Even if we weren't twenty trillion dollars in debt (Thank You to the failed disgusting one party, big state, government, authoritarian establishment for that), even if we had a balanced budget right now. Even if everything was perfect in America and there were no problems, why should socialists get to rob from the taxpayers to redistribute how they choose? The idea itself is egotistical, narcissistic, vain, conceited, self-absorbed, greedy, and unethical to its very core. Many other headaches, problems, and nightmares grow out of the disease that is socialism. Like a sickly fast-spreading fungus, government run health care expands. It takes over everything. It runs your damn life. We've SEEN this and lived through it. Why is this so difficult for the left to understand. Chicken-necked government bureaucrats running your healthcare? Authoritarian tyrants in charge of your body?

We're on a planet floating in space, filled with endless wonder and beauty. All the power of God and the Universe. Yet, humanity itself is under attack. It doesn't mean all patriots and freedom loving people, and myself, and President Trump, and infowars.com, and drudgereport.com, and breitbart.com, and other real human beings have all the answers. It just means that a bunch of authoritarian socialists running every aspect of your life 24/7/365 is not the answer. In this chapter, we will investigate the history of socialism. I'll explain "contemporary socialist politics" around the Earth in places such as Africa, Asia, Europe, the Caribbean, South America, and right here in America. We'll look into what "democratic socialism" is. We'll discuss how socialism and anarchism are one in the same. I'll help the left understand the blatantly obvious truth of why socialized medicine, supported by socialists, is evil. Finally, we'll look at some of the things going on in socialist cities and countries around the world right now, and I'll make the case as to why we have a moral obligation to call out these socialists more than we currently do.

Henri de Saint-Simon was a French aristocrat. He was the creator of the term "socialism." Born in 1760 to a wealthy family, Saint-Simon was very ambitious. He made his valet wake him up every morning with the words "Remember, monsieur le comte, that you have great things to do." One of his early ambitions was to connect the Pacific and Atlantic Oceans through canals. By the time the French Revolution arrived in 1789, he was 29 years old. During the time of violence, he was put in jail based on suspicions that he was connected to counter-revolution activities. He was eventually freed in 1794, and Saint-Simon discovered he made a lot of money because of currency depreciation. Unfortunately for him, his fortune was stolen by his business partner. Saint-Simon decided to spend his time concentrating on political studies. He also began writing and would get a plethora of things published over the span of a couple decades. His term "socialism" was created to counteract "individualism." He eventually got depressed because of what he saw as a lack of social improvement in the world. In 1823 he attempted suicide. Astonishingly, he shot himself in the head SIX times and still didn't die, although he lost vision in one of his eyes. He eventually died in 1825. His works never got enormous attention when he was alive. Saint-Simon's writings and opinions gained much more attention after he died. Eventually, his ideas would come to known as "utopian socialism." By the time the 20th century rolled around, those ideas had spread and gained traction. Socialist parties and groups were getting more influence and power in their various countries. Some of them include the Argentinian Socialist Party, the Russian Social Democratic Labour Party, the Spanish Socialist Workers' Party, Socialist groups in France, the Italian Socialist Party, and of course the Socialist Party of America.

There was massive suffering, bloodshed, violence, and revolution in Russia as the country moved from the old monarch system to a socialist/communist state. Vladimir Lenin said "Long live the world socialist revolution!" as the Russian Socialist Federative Soviet Republic was formed. This was the world's first constitutionally socialist state. In Germany, Hitler took control of the Nazi's, The National Socialist German Workers' Party. That's right, the Nazi's were SOCIALISTS. Many in the propaganda media and the left try to call President Trump Hitler or attempt to intermix Nazis and the American right-wing. The Nazi's weren't right wing, they were socialists. Just because the Nazi's disliked other forms of communism, attacked Russia, and disliked other international forms of socialism, doesn't mean that they weren't still socialists themselves. They were. Again, they were the National Socialist Party. It's time for the media and the left to recognize that today. It's also time for the press and the left to recognize all the countless millions who have died because of socialism.

Cancer from this dangerous and failed ideology has only spread more since the early 20th century. Now, basically, all of Europe is socialist, especially with the dictatorial/anti-freedom European Union. So, Europeans have to deal with their own governments that are either socialist or geared towards socialism, and they also have to deal with the EU which is also tyrannical. They get hit from all directions.

African socialism dominates that continent as well. Julius Nyerere, the first President of Tanzania, was driven by collectivist principles. He firmly believed not only in collectivism but also that Africans were already socialists even before European colonialists came there. Asia is very collectivist, with many forms of communism and socialism. Malaysia elected its first member of Parliament from the Socialist Party of Malaysia, following an election there in 2008. South America, is yet another entire continent dominated by failed socialism. So much of the world deals with this garbage, sadly. Chile, Venezuela, Nicaragua, Bolivia, Ecuador, Brazil, Argentina, and many others are either outright socialist or have incredibly strong socialist influence. The same goes for Central America and the Caribbean. In North America, Canadians consider themselves kind and gentle people participating in democracy. They are very politically correct, and the socialist movement in Canada is powerful. That just leaves us. The United States.

We literally just had a failed president go two full terms without a single year of reaching 3% GDP growth. He screwed us all by socializing medicine through the federal government with Obamacare. Government run, socialized healthcare destroying the life and soul of America. Premiums quadrupling in price. Loss of coverage. Lower Quality all around. No choice what so ever. Socialized medicine is used to control people. You control people's health, and you control them. You control them, and they can't stop your political agenda.

Bernie Sanders, a lifelong government clown, who would not be able to survive in the private sector, had millions of supporters. Political correctness is out of control. Radical leftists regularly cause violence and threaten to kill President Trump. Incompetent, liberal morons in Congress are totally disconnected from any sense of reality. They refuse to accept any responsibility for their disastrous policies or the suffering they cause.

Millions supported Bernie Sanders for President of the United States of America. They supported a socialist. A SOCIALIST. That's the level of insanity going on in our country because of the failed establishment. Sanders described himself as a 'democratic socialist' which was just a way to not sound as radical. He's been in government almost his entire life, and wouldn't even know where to begin in the private sector. Yet, he has multiple homes and expensive sports cars. He is a wealthy white man. He was right about bad trade deals hurting the US, and he is right about wealth inequality, but his ideas would have been a total failure and would have raised taxes to a level that is unimaginable. His energy plan would have been radical. Energy costs would have gone through the roof, while China continues to burn dirty coal. He was also spineless about the fact that he was competing in an openly rigged primary. It was rigged against him, and he was too weak to stop it. He allowed activists to take his microphone away from him in a pathetic display of cowardice as well. He railed against wall street, then after he lost his primary, he supported Hillary Clinton, the biggest Wall Street, Goldman Sachs candidate ever. What a joke. He and Hillary are both Losers and always will be.

There is so much violence coming from the left. They want anarchy. Socialism is an ideology based on theft, so it's only natural that so much violence originates from these insane leftist groups. Radicals throwing bags of human urine, feces, bags of Clorox which can blind you, rocks, eggs, glass bottles, trash, and just straight up hitting people in the face. The violence we witnessed during President Trump's inauguration was shameful. It wasn't like that at Trump rallies. I was there. It was about peace, optimism, strength, hope, freedom, excitement, Love, reviving the American Dream, bringing back prosperity and safety, and of course 'Making America Great Again.' Maybe instead of just insulting, attacking, and smearing people, some of these leftists should have come to some Trump events, and they would have witnessed that for themselves.

Right now, chaos and suffering is happening all over the world because of socialism. Violence in socialist Portland here in America. Mob violence paid for by George Soros. Protests going on in South America.

You may have noticed this chapter is called Venezuela. That's because recently I read a Breitbart article entitled "Maduro Diet: 3 Out of 4 Venezuelans Lost At Least 19 Pounds in 2016" and includes images of impoverished people rummaging through bags of trash looking for anything left that is still edible.[1] That's socialism. Vast human suffering, pain, hunger, and sadness.[2] They eat the zoo animals. They eat the pigeons in the city. They beg the government for scraps. The people of Venezuela starve while tyrant Nicolás Maduro lives in palaces and gets fabulously wealthy.

We have a moral obligation to call out socialists, including both their idiot leaders and their sheep followers. It's not about hurting their feelings. It's about making them realize what their ideas turn into. It's been tried over and over and over again all over the world, and it always fails. It's always a total authoritarian nightmare that destroys the economy, freedom, and everything else. Currently, we're too soft on socialists and are too afraid to hurt their feelings. We let them go on offense, and we stay on defense. The next time you see a socialist, be peaceful, but let them know the suffering socialism causes and maybe if we're lucky we can wake a few of them up, at least some of the ones that aren't totally brainwashed and still have a soul. Tell them you don't like watching people starve. Tell them you want freedom, not authoritarianism. Tell them to earn their own money.

Twelve

Central Banks

What are central banks? What is their history? What do they do? How are they connected to globalism? What are the largest central banks in the world? What is the point of the Federal Reserve System and what are the things people should know about its history? What is the world bank? What is the International Monetary Fund? What is the history of the World Trade Organization, and how has it hurt the United States? What is the history of Goldman Sachs and what should people know about them? Why do the big banks always get bailed out even if they make big mistakes? We'll answer all these questions and more. George Carlin used to say "The game is rigged," but what exactly do the super elites do to give themselves advantages that the rest of us "little people" don't experience. This chapter is about money. It's about crony-capitalism. We'll discuss central banks, international organizations that influence trade/money/currency, and groups like Goldman Sachs who support Hillary.

A central bank is an organization that directs a country's money supply, interest rates, and the currency. Central banks have a monopoly of power in terms of affecting the total amount of money in circulation. The money supply is manipulated through interest rates, adjusted by the central bank. They can also lower reserve requirements, which means banks can make more loans, and thus increase the overall amount of money in the country's economy. Mayer Amschel Rothschild was the founder of the Rothschild Banking dynasty who said: "Give me control of a nation's money supply, and I care not who makes its laws".[1] This power to control money is used against the "little people" and is treacherous in nature. Henry Ford knew the dangers of central banking when he said: "It is well enough that people of the nation do not understand our banking and monetary system, for if they did, I believe there would be a revolution before tomorrow morning."[2]

Rothschild brothers in London wrote to some associates in New York way back in 1863 and told them "The few who understand the system will either be so interested in its profits or be so dependent upon its favours that there will be no opposition from that class, while on the other hand, the great body of people, mentally incapable of comprehending the tremendous advantage that capital derives from the system, will bear its burdens without complaint, and perhaps without even suspecting that the system is inimical to their interests."[3]

Central banks are horrible for a whole array of reasons. First of all, they are totally private. Central banks are private corporations that make their own policies. Decisions are not made based on elections or the best interest of the people. The decisions are based on private interests and made by a private institution. The central bank doesn't just supply the government with money, free of charge. It LOANS it to them and charges interest. After that, they can increase or decrease the amount of money to regulate the very value of the "legal tender" being created. They can control the value of money. This entire system creates one thing. You know what that one thing is? Debt! Lots and lots of debt. Here's how the corrupt fraud works. The Fed produces a dollar bill which is loaned at interest, which means it's equal to $1 plus a percentage of debt based on that dollar. Also, remember the central bank has a monopoly over the money production and is a private entity. Since every dollar has debt already attached to it...where does the money to pay for that debt come from? The money originates from the Central Bank again! This, in turn, creates even more debt. It's a vicious, never-ending cycle of creating more and more debt, and debt is evil. Debt is nothing more than slavery. America's founding fathers understood how bad central banks were hundreds of years ago. Here are a few Quotes from Thomas Jefferson on the subject:

"If the American people ever allow private banks to control the issue of their currency, first by inflation, then by deflation, the banks...will deprive the people of all property until their children wake-up homeless on the continent their fathers conquered.... The issuing power should be taken from the banks and restored to the people, to whom it properly belongs."[4]

"... The modern theory of the perpetuation of debt has drenched the earth with blood, and crushed its inhabitants under burdens ever accumulating."

"I believe that banking institutions are more dangerous to our liberties than standing armies."

James Madison said this "History records that the moneychangers have used every form of abuse, intrigue, deceit, and violent means possible to maintain their control over governments by controlling money and its issuance."

Then there was Woodrow Wilson, who, foolishly, did not listen to the founding fathers' advice. Wilson made the mistake of signing the

1913 Federal Reserve Act. Wilson later recognized what an enormous error he made:

> "I am a most unhappy man. I have unwittingly ruined my country. A great industrial nation is controlled by its system of credit. Our system of credit is concentrated. The growth of the nation, therefore, and all our activities are in the hands of a few men. We have come to be one of the worst ruled, one of the most completely controlled and dominated Governments in the civilized world no longer a Government by free opinion, no longer a Government by conviction and the vote of the majority, but a Government by the opinion and duress of a small group of dominant men."

Another reason central banks are dangerous is they push citizens to a breaking point. Just look at the poverty, homelessness, tension in our country. America has tens of trillions of debt. That's not just the official national debt of about $20 Trillion dollars, but many economists and analysts agree that America's real debt is at least more than three times that. When you add up all the unfunded liabilities, pensions, and an ever-growing government. The middle class is being pushed to annihilation. What's left of the once great American middle class now hangs by a thread. The country's infrastructure is crumbling. There's a lack of competition and monopolies that dominate every market. There is no real competition.

The central banks and the powerful banking interest have done fine though. The globalists have gotten even richer. The globalists love central banking. Globalism and Central Banks are both about consolidation of control, it's no coincidence that so many globalist families have ties to banking. It's about dominating you completely in every way by taking away your free speech, making you suffer economically, and taking away your free will. It's about slavery, a modern-day form of it where you work to please the central banks.

Benjamin Franklin knew this all too well. There were many causes for the revolutionary war against Great Britain. One of them was the fact that King George III outlawed the interest-free, independent, colonial currency that the colonists were using for themselves, forcing them to borrow money from the Central Bank of England instead. This put the colonies into debt and charged them interest. Early American currency went through different stages of development. Different colonies had different systems and were not always equal. For example, a Massachusetts pound was not equal to a Pennsylvania pound. Paper bills were issued which were called "Bills of Credit." Pennsylvania's paper currency was secured by land and experts say that it mainly kept its value when measured against gold, from the time span of 1723 until 1775 when the war broke out. There were also incredible amounts of commodity trading going on at that point. People would trade furs, skins, tobacco, farming tools, fabric, cloth, fish, wheat, corn, livestock, sugar, beef, pork, cotton, lumber, coal, rice, maple syrup, copper, and many other things. It's not that the commodity system was perfect or the colonial money was perfect, it's that it was independent and free. It was unique. The British Parliament started passing Currency Acts. These Currency Acts were enacted in 1751, 1764, and 1773 and their purpose was to regulate colonial paper money. It was about control. Benjamin Franklin said that: "The refusal of King George III to allow the colonies to operate an honest money system, which freed the ordinary man from the clutches of the money manipulators, was probably the prime cause of the revolution."[5]

The revolution started and we know the rest. America won its freedom. The United States Declaration of Independence was signed. Years after that, in 1787, the US Constitution was signed at

Independence Hall in Philadelphia, Pennsylvania. We were free from England. Sadly, our beloved country's battle with central banks and the selfish men who associate with them was not over. It was just beginning.

Flash forward to the early 20th century. The wealthy, big business/banking families included the Rothschilds, the Rockefellers, the Morgans, and a few others. These people pushed for legislation that would once again create a central bank. The public, however, was opposed to such legislation, and they needed to manufacture a crisis to advance the bill. J.P. Morgan abused his influence by writing rumors that an important bank in New York was insolvent. Morgan helped create massive panic. It worked. People feared to lose their deposits, which caused a bunch of withdrawals. Other banks were affected as well. The panic spread. Banks had to start calling in most of their loans, causing a frenzy of bankruptcies and repossessions. This financial crisis was known as the 'Panic of 1907' and is also sometimes referred to as the '1907 Banker's Panic'. There was a three-week stretch that was absolutely hellish for investors. The New York Stock Exchange fell roughly 50% from where it was just a year prior. The small bankers were hurt badly and most lost everything. The elite bankers got what they wanted, though. The Panic had created a crisis of confidence in the system. Frederick Allen was a historian who explained this in Life Magazine saying "The Morgan interests took advantage… to precipitate the panic (of 1907), guiding it shrewdly as it progressed." A few years later, the elite bankers met in secret to write their new legislation. They wanted a central bank so badly, they were practically salivating. The central banking bill, called the Federal Reserve Act, was written. It's important for folks to understand that this was written by BANKERS, not lawmakers. Senator Nelson Aldrich, who had deep connections with banking interests and eventually married into the Rockefeller family, also wanted a central bank. Aldrich was used as a front-man to push the bill through Congress.[6] In 1913, Woodrow Wilson became the President, with his aide from the bankers. Wilson agreed to sign the Federal Reserve Act because of a deal which gave him campaign support. The Act was voted in, and President Wilson made it law. The Federal Reserve Banking Organization was open for business.[7] What a hideous decision he made. The American people were lied played. Over the years, even more, small banks went out of business. The elites wanted their competition done away with. Thousands of smaller banks crumbled. The monopolies were getting even stronger. Louis McFadden was a Republican congressman from Pennsylvania who was a stalwart critic of the Federal Reserve System. The congressman was a brave man who took a bold stand and said that "When the Federal Reserve Act was passed, the people of these United States did not perceive that a world banking system was being set up here. A super-state controlled by international bankers and industrialists acting together to enslave the world for their own pleasure. Every effort has been made by the Fed to conceal its powers but the truth is—the Fed has usurped the government!!"[8] A series of even more bankruptcies and consolidation happened. Congressman Charles Lindbergh said "The financial system ... has been turned over to the Federal Reserve Board. That board administers the finance system by authority of ... a purely profiteering group. The system is private, conducted for the sole purpose of obtaining the greatest possible profits from the use of other people's money."[9] and that "From now on, depressions will be scientifically created."[10] The next great panic, in 1920, was nothing compared to what happened in 1929. Margin loans caused another selloff. Yet again, thousands of smaller banks went under, along with some medium-sized businesses. The international, monopolistic bankers came in and bought up entire corporations for pennies on the dollar. They also bought up their rival banks. It was one of the largest heists in world history. The Federal

Reserve only made the situation worse and helped exacerbate what would be known as the "Great Depression." Congressman McFadden attempted to bring impeachment charges against the Fed board. He said "It was not accidental. It was a carefully contrived occurrence.... The international bankers sought to bring about a condition of despair here so that they might emerge as rulers of us all."[11] There was a series of assassination attempts on McFadden's life, and he was poisoned before he could bring the impeachment proceedings further. I think we should honor Congressman McFadden's bravery for standing up to these banking criminals. That was something that took incredible courage. The predatorial elite bankers weren't done, however. It wasn't enough for them that they lowered the American people to poverty, hunger, filth, and total hopelessness. They removed the gold standard.[12] People were required to turn over their gold bullion or go to jail. Dollars bills before 1933 were redeemable by gold. Take a dollar bill out of your wallet or purse and look at it right now. It says it is legal tender. It no longer says it is redeemable in gold. It's backed by nothing at all. It's worthless toilet paper. What's also sick is how these globalist bankers have profited from funding both sides of wars. They love war. When wars break out, the government must borrow more money from them. For these selfish bankers, the profits are extraordinary during wartime. Standard Oil, owned by the Rockefellers, also sold millions of dollars of fuel to a company called I.G. Farben, a company that produced Nazi explosives. The Nazi air force would not have been able to function without an additive which was patented by Standard Oil. There was also the Union Banking Corporation which helped fund Hitler's rise to power and was a Nazi money laundering bank. Prescott Bush, the father of George H.W. Bush, and grandfather of George W. Bush was one of the founders of this bank and even served as a director of it. The Union Banking Corporation was shut down, and its assets were seized by the U.S. Government under the U.S. Trading with the Enemy Act. This is how seditious and evil some of these banking interests really are. They know they can do anything they want. The Federal Reserve was a dreadful creation that only made these powerful, arrogant elites more ruthless. Just remember this quote from the great Barry Goldwater who said "Most Americans have no real understanding of the operation of the international moneylenders. The accounts of the Federal Reserve System have never been audited. It operates outside the control of Congress and manipulates the credit of the United States."

So, what other central banks are out there other than the Federal Reserve? First, there's the Bank of England. Most central banks are based on the Bank of England. It was established in 1694 and was one of the original central banks, although it didn't have many of the powers that modern central banks have today. The Bank of Amsterdam was created in 1609 and presented the very first international reserve currency, which was called the bank guilder/Dutch guilder. The Bank of Sweden was established in 1668, and its management was initially chosen by the King at that time. Next, we have the European Central Bank, ECB, set up in 1998, which sprung out of the European Union. The ECB's objective is to "maintain price stability".[13] There is also the People's Bank of China, the Central Bank of Brazil, the Central Bank of Ireland, and many others.

Aside from Central Banks, other powerful organizations need to be discussed. The first is the International Monetary Fund, IMF, which was created in 1945. The IMF headquarters is in Washington D.C. and on the IMF website it says that "The International Monetary Fund (IMF) is an organization of 189 countries, working to foster global monetary cooperation, secure financial stability, facilitate international trade, promote high employment and sustainable economic growth, and reduce poverty around the world."[14] Let's evaluate this statement. Has it fostered global monetary cooperation? The answer is no. If it did, the Communist Chinese government would not devalue their currency and rip us off the way they do. Has it secured financial stability? The answer is no. Tens of millions of Americans struggle just to survive. There are homeless veterans, not enough good jobs, taxes are too high, and not enough Americans are currently living the American dream. Has it facilitated international trade? Yes, it has helped facilitate rigged trade deals that hurt the United States and benefits our competitors. Has it promoted high employment and sustainable economic growth? Not in America. Has it reduced poverty around the world? Not in America it hasn't, poverty is still way too high here; and considering most of the world is either socialist or communist I would say they've failed worldwide as well.

The World Trade Organization, WTO, was founded in 1995 and is headquartered in Geneva, Switzerland.[15] The WTO has been a catastrophe for America. Everyone else's interests come before ours. Why was China allowed to enter the WTO? To hurt the United States economically, that's why. Maybe the WTO has benefited other nations, but it hasn't benefited us, that's for sure. Jobs shipped overseas. Factories closed. Manufacturing made exponentially more challenging. An American economy left with nothing. Everyone eating America's lunch. Everyone ripping us off. Everyone laughs at us while they profit from deals that hurt us. What a disgrace.

The World Bank was established in 1945, and its headquarters is in Washington D.C. where they claim to have the goal of reducing poverty.[16] Again, has poverty been reduced in America? NO! All of these globalist organizations have failed. And to make matters worse; our taxes are too damn high domestically. The middle class is getting slaughtered alive with taxes. It's out of control. The IRS is filled with a bunch of criminals. They target conservatives and the Tea Party, and there are no consequences. So many tea party groups literally targeted by the IRS for their political beliefs and the propaganda media has long moved on. One of my favorite authors, Wayne Allyn Root, was targeted by the IRS for his political beliefs. Absolutely ridiculous. Many other conservatives were targeted. The IRS needs to shut down. People guilty of crimes in the IRS need to be prosecuted. Taxes need to be lowered drastically on the middle class. It's really not complicated. You have all these super wealthy people keeping their money offshore. Cut the taxes across the board on everyone in America, and they can bring that money back here and invest. President Trump's tax cut proposals are fantastic, but we need to eventually go even beyond that and cut them even more. This includes getting rid of capital gains taxes which hurt economic growth and stifle our economy.

Since we talked about Central Banks earlier, we should talk about Goldman Sachs. Goldman Sachs is not technically a central bank, but it is very powerful. Goldman Sachs is a multinational investment banking company. Goldman Sachs always seems to find a way to get their people in government. It's inevitable. They have a lot of money, and therefore they always have tremendous influence and power. Goldman Sachs banned their employees from donating to Trump in the election.[17] Donating to Hillary Clinton was all right though. 100% of Goldman Sachs money went to Hillary Rodham Clinton. It's ok though, she's going to protect you from Wall Street. What a sick joke. She was THE Wall Street candidate. Goldman Sachs even issues a statement saying they can't donate to the Trump/Pence ticket because Mike Pence was still the Governor of Indiana and that would be unethical. Give me a break. They released that statement for a reason, folks. That was about throwing it in your face. That was about mocking you. That was about them telling you, hey we're Goldman Sachs, and we'll do whatever the hell we want. That was them telling the American people that they're stupid and go back to sleep now. Think back to the financial crisis of 2008. Who got bailed out? The Banks did, of course. Bailouts are un-American. Bush supported bailouts.

Obama supported bailouts. The Senate passed a $700 billion-dollar bank bailout bill in 2008. Just thinking about it makes me want to physically throw up. People sitting there like Lloyd Blankfein, Jamie Dimon, and a bunch of other bankers. I'm so sick of these weak, selfish, stupid bankers. They don't care about you. They don't give a damn about the middle class or the working people who make their lives possible. If they cared as much about the middle-class profits as they do their own, then the middle-class would be doing much better. It's that simple. They only care about themselves. The point is, the American people need to wake the hell up. We need to discuss how bad the Federal Reserve is. We need to talk about how badly we've been ripped off by globalist organizations. We need to have real competition so we can compete with the existing monopolies that exist in Big Pharma, the Telecom companies, Media, the Insurance industry, Google, Facebook, YouTube, Twitter, and a bunch more. They hate competition. They hate free speech. In order to 'Make America Great Again,' we have to compete against the monopolies which in turn will create more choice, freedom, better quality, lower prices, and more diversity of thought.

Thirteen

ISIS

Radical Islam is nothing but a dangerous cancer on humanity. It's real. It's barbaric and very lethal. It's demonic. It hates humanity. It wants to kill us. It's long past time for the media and the left to recognize the threat that is out there. Radical Islamic terrorists don't care whether you're conservative, liberal, libertarian, green party, democrat, republican, straight, gay, lesbian, black, white, Hispanic, short, tall, rich, poor, well educated, less than well educated, have a nice car, have a crappy car, if you're from the city, if you're from a rural area, or anything else. They hate all of us. They hate freedom, and they hate America. Period. It also doesn't matter what religion you believe in, or if you chose not to believe. They want us to be their slaves. They want us to submit to their insanity. They want to torture us. They want to cut off our heads. I know that this is pretty complicated stuff for the failed propaganda media and for the left but try and follow along. When something demonic wants to cut off your head, you have to first, A) Acknowledge that it exists; and B) Call it out by name; before you can finally C) Have a plan to defeat it. I'm thankful that we have a President who isn't afraid to name the enemy. He understands the threat, acknowledges it, and calls them out directly. All that's remaining is the final result, which is to eradicate them from the planet. That plan must defeat them both militarily and ideologically. It isn't enough to just defeat them in battle. We must also totally discredit their failed, barbaric ideology from the fifth century. The fifth century was a brutal time. We don't want to go back to that. In this chapter we'll discuss the history of radical Islam over the centuries, including how vile, oppressive, murderous, and evil it truly is. We'll also examine the chaos that is going on right now. First, here are some must read Quotes about Radical Islam:

"In our towns and cities they will continue to be born, in our communities they will go on to be nurtured & radicalized & from within our neighborhoods they will terrorize & murder our citizens including women & children in their attempt to destroy the very fabric & order of our civilized society. They are influenced by our ignorance, our lack of knowledge is their power, martyrdom in the name of their God and prophet is their aspiration & so it is critical that we waste no time & learn more about them & this ideology they follow before we can even begin to eradicate this chilling & growing endemic Islamic faith based terrorism'." [1]

—CAL SARWAR, AUTHOR

"The secular elites are so terrified of telling the truth about radical Islam. When you talk about the radical Islamists, we have got to get straight and get serious and talk about it in the right way."[2]

—NEWT GINGRICH, AUTHOR, FORMER SPEAKER OF THE HOUSE

"To speak specifically of our problem with the Muslim world, we are meandering into a genuine clash of civilizations, and we're deluding ourselves with euphemisms. We're talking about Islam being a religion of peace that's been hijacked by extremists. If ever there were a religion that's not a religion of peace, it is Islam."[3]

—SAM HARRIS, AUTHOR, NEUROSCIENTIST

"They have a Twitter account up today, ISIS does, about turning the United States into a "river of blood" if it comes in and tries to defend the city of Baghdad. And trust me, that is going to come to Europe. That is going to come to Central Europe, it's going to come to Western Europe, it's going to come to the United Kingdom. And so I think we are in a crisis of the underpinnings of capitalism, and on top of that we're now, I believe, at the beginning stages of a global war against Islamic fascism."[4]

—STEPHEN BANNON, WHITE HOUSE CHIEF STRATEGIST

"We are foolish not to accept the fact mosques, whether in Muslim-majority countries or not, feed Islam's followers with hate messages for non-Muslims. So fed, some opt to radicalize and act on them; some do not. But we need understand terrorism emanates from such hate speech against non-Muslims. Because Islam's foundation is built upon this hatred, it is not extremists who have hijacked Islam to give it a violent interpretation; it is moderates who have hijacked Islam to give it a non-violent one."[5]

—LT. COL. JAMES ZUMWALT

"When the enemy says they're jihadists, you don't get to call them unemployed disenfranchised individuals who need a better education. We have to prosecute this war objectively and understand the enemy as they understand themselves."[6]

—DR. SEBASTIAN GORKA, DEPUTY ASSISTANT TO PRESIDENT TRUMP

"The idea that federal agencies, armed services, and law enforcement are not allowed to discuss the religious motivation and ideology of our enemies, and that words such as jihad have to be censored out of our lexicon of counter-terrorism and military training has to end."

—DR. SEBASTIAN GORKA, DEPUTY ASSISTANT TO PRESIDENT TRUMP

Before we talk about Islam's radical history, let's talk about just a few of the many things that have been going on in the present. There was an article on dailywire.com in early September 2016 called "'Violent Torture Tools' Found in ISIS Prison For Female Sex Slaves [Video], " and it included a video which was difficult to watch.[7] An abandoned ISIS prison was found where female sex slaves were held and tortured. The women were fed leftovers which were disgustingly thrown on the dirty floor. They had to drink out of dog bowls that were filled with the most revolting, stomach-churning water one could possibly imagine. There were no mattresses. They were trapped in solitary cages. It was the worst torture you could fathom. The article discussed how women were beaten and punched in the stomach to kill the unborn children who were conceived through rape. These are the kinds of sick animals we're up against.

Think back to just as recently as Christmas time, 2016. Remember the evil Berlin Truck attack? A third-world barbarian, in a tractor trailer truck, driving over scores of innocent people at a Christmas market.[8] Twelve people lost their lives, and fifty-six others were injured. Imagine the fear these people must have been going through. Imagine what must have been going through their minds in that situation. Let's pray for all of these victims, their friends and families. These poor families will never be the same again. It wasn't an accident that it was an attack during Christmas time. They were sending a deliberate message. A clear message that they will stop at nothing to rid the world of Christianity, goodness, and civilization itself. They will stop at nothing, to cause as much pain, violence, chaos, suffering, and death as they possibly can.[9] We must take the ISIS threat seriously![10]

Islam has been at war with Christians, Jews, and non-Muslims for roughly one and a half millennia. There were many Muslim conquests in the 600's. The Battle of Ajnadayn was a major conflict between the Byzantine Empire and the Arabs. The Muslims had a victory, and their armies took over the Capital city of Damascus in 636. Then there was the Siege of Jerusalem which fell in the 637-638-time frame. Next, the Rashidun Caliphate conquered Alexandria in Egypt. After that, they took control of Persia which led to the downfall of the Sasanian Empire. By the early 700's they were moving closer and closer toward the heart of Europe. In 711, Muslim fighters invaded Hispania, a Visigothic Kingdom. The Visigoths were part of the nomadic, Germanic tribes. King Roderic was the Visigoth King of Hispania. King Roderic attempted to push back the invasion. His forces met directly with the Umayyad Caliphate in the Battle of Guadalete. King Roderic was killed in action, along with most of the Visigoth nobles. Muslim commander Tariq ibn Ziyad was successful. The Visigoth capital, Toledo was overtaken. The Caliphate was getting stronger. Non-Muslims were taken as slaves, beheaded, forced to pay taxes to fund the Caliphate, tortured, and most were just outright killed. Arabs conquered most of the Christian world including Mesopotamia, Syria, Egypt, Spain, North Africa, and the holy land. Eventually, Europeans got tired of these Islamic invaders taking their land and killing them. The middle ages brought the Crusades, which were a series of military expeditions that were managed by Europeans to defend their lands and to defend Christianity.[11] Pope Urban II made a call to arms and said that anyone who fought would be partaking in a sacred act. He said that knights and Crusaders could earn indulgences, which was a way to limit punishment for sins. The Pope also wanted to retake the holy lands such as Jerusalem, which were sacred because it was where Christ had lived and walked. This resonated deeply with many Europeans. Massive numbers of Knights, commoners, and people of all walks of life joined together. There was also a plethora of powerful Lords who merged their armies together for the mission. The Crusaders set out towards the East. This was the First Crusade, 1096-1099. It was incredibly successful. Lands were retaken, most important being Jerusalem. Jerusalem was taken away from the Fatimid Caliphate. The Crusades continued off and on for hundreds of years. Tremendous amounts of blood were spilled, as Christians and Muslims fought each other endlessly. Control of certain lands went back on forth. One of the big turning points was the Industrial Revolution. The Renaissance brought major upgrades in education, healthcare, literacy, art, politics, science, inductive reasoning, self-awareness, and overall culture. The quality of life was starting to improve. There were inventions and/or improvements in things such as gunpowder, the mechanical clock, the printing press, the microscope, blast furnaces, and muskets. By the late 1700's manufacturing was becoming stronger, faster, more efficient, and more powerful. There were new gas lighting utilities that were better than candles which helped factories and stores stay open longer. New machines, often powered by steam and the development of machining tools quickly made the older manufacturing processes of hand production outdated. The industrial revolution began around 1760. There were other improvements in mining, better roads, railways, clothing, consumer goods, and housing. There were also improvements in agricultural technology which increased overall food production and people's nutritional status. As a result of these incredible advances, the population rose rapidly, and so did standards of living. The Europeans could now build much better and stronger armies. The Muslims quickly found themselves with inferior technology, out gunned, out manned, out maneuvered, out strategized, and outsmarted. The Muslims were pushed out of Europe and had lost much of their Islamic Empire lands from centuries past. By 1924, the Islamic Empire ended. By that point, the Islamic Caliphate had been around for more than 1400 years, and Islamists had killed hundreds of millions of non-Muslims by the sword.

What was left of the scattered Caliphate began organizing politically. They were going through an identity crisis. The Muslim Brotherhood was founded in 1928 in Egypt. Its goal was and still is, to re-establish a global Islamic Caliphate. The Muslim Brotherhood believed it was possible to reform society so that sharia law would dominate the world. The Brotherhood wanted to start with individual Muslims and help them regain their fighting edge and have them start standing up for Islamic values. From there, they could then reform entire families, and then society as a whole. After that, they could reform entire states, and eventually, the whole world would be under Islamic control. Their goal was world domination right from the start. They had learned nothing from the past few centuries. The Muslim Brotherhood's founder was Hassan al-Banna who stated that "It is in the nature of Islam to dominate, not to be dominated, to impose its law on all nations and to extend its power to the entire planet."[12] He wanted to rebuild the territorial, religious, and political foundations of the Caliphate and then eventually conquer the world. The Muslim Brotherhood also had ideological connections to Nazism, which was spreading at that time. Grand Mufti Amin al-Husseini was a Muslim leader (who was close to the founder of Muslim Brotherhood) who even met with Hitler in 1941 which proves that Islam and Nazism have similar world views. They believed Germany was going to win WWII. They both saw Jews as enemies, along with the English, French, and Americans. The Brotherhood's motto is "Allah is our objective. The Prophet is our leader. The Qur'an is our law. Jihad is our way.

Dying in the way of Allah is our highest hope. Allahu akbar!" It's logo literally has swords on it. They glorify Osama bid Laden and in 2007 Former Muslim Brotherhood Supreme Guide Muhammed Mahdi Akef said that he is "in all certainty, a mujahid (heroic fighter), and I have no doubt in his sincerity in resisting the occupation, close to Allah on high."

They only care about destroying the United States and Israel. They hate women. They hate freedom. They've always encouraged and vigorously helped to incite violence. They work to help create more terrorist groups and networks. There are even several Muslim countries themselves that have labeled the Muslim Brotherhood a terrorist group. That's because they are. Bahrain, the United Arab Emirates, Saudi Arabia, and Egypt have all listed the Brotherhood as a terrorist organization. This shows there is nothing "anti-Muslim" about labeling them as such. It's time for the United States to recognize the Muslim Brotherhood as the terrorist organization it is.

Aside from the problems the Muslim Brotherhood is causing, so many of these middle eastern countries openly flaunt their desires to destroy America. Countries that publicly fund terrorist organizations, and countries who would love to wipe us off the Earth. The globalists and neocons would love to get us tied down in as many wars as possible. We must avoid war, and should always avoid war. The war in Iraq only further destabilized the region. We lost thousands of brave American heroes and spent trillions of dollars. That money could be better used in the United States. Instead of war, we need Peace through Strength. Peace through Strength means avoiding war by having such a strong defense nobody will want to mess with us. We need to remember what happened on 9/11.[13] It also means we don't go out looking for war just because we have the best military in the world. Part of this means taking these threats seriously and dealing with them in a way which keeps America safer, without getting us into another middle eastern engagement. Additionally, we need to stop letting money and weapons get into the hands of terrorists. Congresswomen Tulsi Gabbard is a Democrat from Hawaii who even introduced a bill called the "Stop Arming Terrorists Act" and is co-sponsored by both democrats and republicans.[14] H.R. 608:

"Stop Arming Terrorists Act
This bill prohibits the use of federal agency funds to provide covered assistance to: (1) Al Qaeda, Jabhat Fateh al-Sham, the Islamic State of Iraq and the Levant (ISIL), or any individual or group that is affiliated with, associated with, cooperating with, or adherents to such groups; or (2) the government of any country that the Office of the Director of National Intelligence (ODNI) determines has, within the most recent 12 months, provided covered assistance to such a group or individual.

"Covered assistance" is defined as:

- defense articles, defense services, training or logistical support, or any other military assistance provided by grant, loan, credit, transfer, or cash sales;
- intelligence sharing; or
- cash assistance.**"**

We also must be aware of the unholy alliance between globalists and radical Islam. Globalists want to use radical Islam as their foot soldiers to destabilize the United States and Europe to bring in more government control. What do globalists and Islamic terrorists have in common? They both hate Christianity.[15] They both hate freedom. They both hate America and Europe. They both want to dissolve countries and sovereignty. They both want to cause chaos. They want to create chaos for different purposes mind you, radical Islam wants a new caliphate like they had 1,000 years ago, and the globalists want chaos to bring in more global governance and controls, so they have different goals, but in the meantime, they both have a mutual interest in causing problems. It's difficult to know just exactly how many countries ISIS is operating in right now, but whatever the answer is, it's still too many. I think it's important to degrade ISIS as much as humanly possible. These are stupid, barbaric, third-world, barn-animals, who worship death and evil. They're very slow, unintelligent, imbecile, simpleminded, failures, and morons. They can, must, and will lose. We will win. I spit on ISIS and their failed caliphate. I openly laugh at how unintelligent they are. They actually believe they can reestablish a caliphate. They're losers and pure garbage. ISIS is trash who can look forward to a total defeat, and then they can enjoy eternity in hell.

Fourteen

Obama's Legacy

Barack Hussein Obama II was the worst President in the history of the United States of America. He will be remembered as the first president EVER to NOT REACH 3% GDP growth in eight years (it's now been more than a decade without 3% growth when we should be at at least double that rate every year). He will be remembered as a petty, spoiled tyrant who selfishly used his status as America's first black president, to be totally above the law and disrespect the American people at every turn. He will be remembered for doubling the national debt, creating Trillions and Trillions of debts for future generations. Obama referred to people in small towns in Pennsylvania as bitter clingers, people who cling to guns and religion.[1] I'm from a small town in Pennsylvania. They're not bitter clingers, they're people who've been abused by their own federal government for decades. They're people who have been lied to, swindled, robbed, and exploited by the political establishment of both parties for a very, very long time. The bitter clinger is Barack Obama. He bitterly clings to his hatred, lies, deceit, government control, selfishness, incompetence, and absolute disdain for the people he was supposed to be working for. His legacy is pure fraud. His legacy is tyranny. His legacy is lawlessness. I will give Obama credit though; he was one of the most successful con men in history.

His failed Legacy is one of ignorance, authoritarianism, hatred, corruption, globalism, contempt for our Founding Fathers, contempt for the U.S. Constitution, and contempt for freedom. His legacy is about exorbitantly high taxes, enormous increases in poverty, a crumbling infrastructure, decaying civil liberties, and viciously assaulting the fabric of our country. His legacy is about taking freedom away from the people. The people are supposed to be in charge, the government is supposed to work for us. Obama's world is about slavery. It's about making the American people slaves to government and globalism. It's about Cloward-Piven, overloading the system with spending/entitlements/debt/welfare/food stamps on purpose to give power to the government.[2] It's about literally putting the Federal Government in charge of your healthcare and taking that away from you as well. It's about golf, vacations, and getting nothing done while working class people struggle to survive. It's about pushing a bunch of cultural garbage and bringing ignorant people like Lebron James and Rick Ross to the White House.[3] It's about a third world economy in America.[4] It's about getting money from George Soros. It's about not being able to say radical Islam.[5] It's about having a CIA director, John O. Brennan, a man who refused to be sworn in on a Bible. A CIA director who once voted for the Communist Party candidate for President, has deep ties to Islam, and who told President Trump to watch his mouth. Brennan is someone with deep Saudi connections and just looks like a classic villain. A former CIA director who is an absolute embarrassment.

Humanity can do infinitely better than Obama. Obama's Legacy is about scandals, cover-ups, criminality, dishonesty, and indignation.

In this chapter, we'll examine Obama's many scandals, and I'll try not to leave any out. After that, I'll make the case as to why Barack Obama should be dragged in front of Grand Juries multiple times, and why Obama should be prosecuted for his multitude of crimes and offenses.

Everyone on planet Earth knows the Obamacare lies that we were told. If you like your plan, you'll be able to keep your healthcare plan.[6] If you like your doctor, you'll be able to keep your doctor. We're going to lower premiums by thousands of dollars per family per year. No family making less than $250,000 a year will see their taxes increase.[7] Obamacare will be fiscally responsible. Not a dime will be added to our deficits, not now or in the future.[8] Every American will be covered. Deductibles will go down. The healthcare.gov website will work great. Emergency room visits will go down substantially.[9] These are all pure lies. 100% pure, old-fashioned, solid grade, fraud. Jonathan Gruber was one of the architects of the failure, who later said a "lack of transparency" and the "stupidity of the American voter" helped Obamacare get passed. "Lack of transparency is a huge political advantage," Gruber explained, "And basically, call it the stupidity of the American voter or whatever, but basically that was really, really critical for the thing to pass."[10] Tens of millions have been left without health insurance. Obamacare has added trillions to the long-term deficit. Obamacare had at least 18 new taxes. Millions have been hit with double-digit premium hikes every year since it pushed through. Premiums up 116% in Arizona. Slaughtering the middle class. A huge chunk of our country literally only has one health insurance option. No choice what so ever. Millions can't see their preferred doctor. Millions had their plans canceled. Make no mistake. Obama knew this would happen. This is the result they wanted. It gave them more governmental control. When the government can affect your health care, they've got full control of your life. It created a rigged, monopoly insurance industry. It was a federal government run, socialized medicine nightmare that makes me want to throw up.

Obama's economic record is hard to put into words. If you think of the American economy as some guy walking down the street. Obama basically walked up to that guy, "economically" hit him over the back with a baseball bat, punched him in the face, put shards of glass in his eye, punched his teeth out, took his health care away, taxed him, regulated him, made his country more dangerous, called him a racist, robbed him, laughed at him, demonized him, and hit him a few more times as he was trying to get up. And no, I'm not literally saying Obama physically attacked anyone. It's abstract. It's a simile. It's metaphysical. It's what he spiritually did to our economy, and what he did through his policies. Close to 100 Million Americans out of work. That's not an accident. That's purposely putting people on government assistance so that the government becomes more needed and more powerful. More business closing every day than opening each day. Household family incomes down. Tens of millions on food stamps. Taxes killing everything. Regulations killing economic activity and entrepreneurial spirit in general. EPA out of control. The U.S. Department of Labor putting out fraudulent unemployment numbers to try and make it look like things were better than they really were. I even sent a letter to the Secretary of Labor, Thomas Perez last year which told them their unemployment numbers were false and I outlined, using facts/data/graphs/charts, why those numbers are actually much higher. They knew they were false, but I think it's important to not be bullied or intimidated by this trash, folks. Don't be afraid to stand up to them, peacefully, using your first amendment. Thomas Perez is now the DNC chairman. Good luck, schmuck. The Obama economy was hell on Earth. It was suffering for hard working people.

What was Obama doing while this suffering was going on? Golfing. Lots and Lots of Golfing. Golfchannel.com has an article by Ryan

Reiterman from January 20, 2017, that explained this. Apparently, the final tally for Obama was 333 rounds of golf as President of the United States of America. Most Americans can't go golfing. They can't afford golf clubs. They can barely afford food. There were also the Obama vacations, which cost taxpayers more than money. We lost, even more, respect around the world. We have homeless Veterans starving in the streets of America and this jackass just goes on endless vacations and tries to delegitimize President Trump and the American people. Of course, he went to Hawaii over Christmas time of 2016, into 2017. Step one: Insert the "Countering Disinformation And Propaganda Act" into the NDAA thus making it law, which puts a 'Ministry of Truth' administrative board in charge of free speech in America and makes us a third world country. Check. Step two: Go on a 17 day Hawaiian Vacation, funded by taxpayers, walk on stunning white sand beaches, require a bunch of secret service agents around you, rent a multi-million-dollar beachfront home, living the good life like a King, on other peoples' money. Check

Obama's Justice Department was just another politicized fraud. There was no rule of law what so ever. Obama's all about the law of the Jungle, baby. Remember, Eric Holder? How could you not? What a piece of garbage. Loretta Lynch recently called for more marching, blood, and death on the streets. This woman was recently the Attorney General of the United States. Our nation's top cop. She oversaw the United States Department of Justice. Think about that for a minute. This was the Obama minion who met with Bill Clinton on a tarmac.[11] The meeting happened in Phoenix, while Hillary was under investigation (and should still be) by the FBI.[12] What a disgusting human being and Bill Clinton is still a rapist as well. This was the Obama Justice department. Wasn't it nauseating the way they involved themselves in every case between a police officer and some criminal who tried to attack the police? The JUSTICE DEPARTMENT undermining…. the police. It was about racial division and still is. That's what they love. Racial tensions and racially divided us. Attorney Generals who think they are social justice warriors. Get people thinking about tribalism. Make it about skin color, instead of us all just being Americans. A strategy as old as time: Divide and Conquer. There was also a shadowy, secretive DOJ slush fund as well. Obama was funneling billions of dollars through the DOJ and into liberal groups. This is according to congress's own congressional investigators. DOJ bureaucrats using your tax dollars for their own personal desires. An Obama banana republic. That's what we were, folks. That's how close we were to losing this country forever. Let's also remember Fast and Furious. In 2010, a U.S. Customs and Border Patrol Agent was on patrol and was killed while on duty. This hero should have never been killed. Two firearms found at the scene were weapons Obama and Holder let walk as part of Operation Fast and Furious. Operation Fast and Furious was a firearm trafficking racket. Roughly 2,000 guns flowed to Mexican cartels, illegally of course. When scumbag, murder, drug-dealer, a piece of street filth "El Chapo" who I hope rots in hell for eternity, was captured (Again) last year. They not only found El Scumbag, but they also found an enormous .50 caliber rifle, a weapon which can stop vehicles and knock down helicopters, which was from the operation.[13] There were more than 30 rifles just like that which were sold in the operation. Thanks, Obama and Holder. Dipshits. The Fast and Furious scandal investigation was immediately stonewalled, just like every fake investigation our government has. Fake investigations that uncover wrongdoings and illegal behavior…and then nothing happens. It's what happens when a bunch of spineless people are in government. The committee subpoenaed relevant documents. Holder refuses to give them over. Nothing happens. If that were some working-class guy, who didn't follow court orders he would be locked up immediately. Eric Holder needs to be dragged in front of Grand Juries, not congressional investigations, GRAND JURIES for his behavior.

Of course, Obama abused the 1917 Espionage Act at a level that is insane. From 1917 to 2008, the Espionage Act was only used three times. Obama used it all the time. He used it more than all previous administrations combined![14] His justice department used it at least nine times by 2015 alone, to charge individuals with espionage. Whistleblowers were charged as well. Tom Drake was a senior executive at the U.S. National Security Agency who became a whistleblower.[15] Drake blew the whistle on an illegal program to collect data/communications on American citizens. He did everything the way you're supposed to do it. He went to all the right people and even to the Congressional Oversight Committee. Drake was charged with ten separate counts and faced five charges under the Espionage Act. All of them were thrown out. They were thrown out after he lost his job, his house, and even his pension. The message is clear. You dig up illegality, fraudulent behavior, abuse of power. etc. and you're the one who has committed a crime, not the elements of the government committing the crimes being exposed.

Journalists were harassed, monitored, and heavily surveilled. James Rosen of Fox News was monitored and labeled a "criminal co-conspirator".[16] Holder signed off on a search warrant of Rosen. Rosen was also labeled a flight risk. Judge Andrew Napolitano said, "This is the first time that the federal government has moved to this level of taking ordinary, reasonable, traditional, lawful reporter skills and claiming they constitute criminal behavior." Everyone is spied on now. That is just the nature of the surveillance state we live in. A surveillance state that Obama only encouraged and grew. The NSA has collection capability on everything you own. Your phone, laptop, emails, texts, social media posts, and everything else. Massive NSA data storage facilities around the country that house multiple zettabytes of information, which includes not just metadata, but also recordings, and data from virtually every type of communication imaginable. Do you know how large a zettabyte is? It is one sextillion bytes or 1,000 exabytes. A zettabyte is equivalent to 62.5 Billion iPhones, or iPhones stacked on top of each other 295, 928 miles high which would go past the moon. One zettabyte is equal to 152 million years of UHD 8K video (ultra-high definition television). 8K High-resolution display has pixels so small they are virtually indistinguishable to the human eye. The government can comfortably house multiple zettabytes, and the global elites are very interested in developing quantum computing which would make even supercomputers irrelevant. How scary is that? Quantum computers that can calculate what you're going to do before you even know yourself. Don't worry though, the government would never do anything wrong.

So, was the government monitoring candidate Donald Trump, President-elect Trump, and President Trump? Is water wet? Is the sky blue? Is grass green? Of course, they were spying on him. They spy on and surveil all of us. Trump was surveilled, spied on, and that information was dissected to see how he could be politically targeted with it. His transition team was targeted as well. Lt. General Michael Flynn was targeted and his rights were violated. This is what happens when you have somebody like Donald J Trump who was against the Iraq war. He's against globalism and horrible trade deals which have ripped us off. He's against incompetent, weak, corrupt, unintelligent government people who have run the country into the ground. He's always been critical of the government, including the Democrat establishment, Republican establishment, and the globalist establishment.

Dr. Jerome Corsi is a New York times bestselling author multiple times, who has been doing a fantastic job breaking huge stories, despite the mainstream media ignoring them. He and others have discovered that Trump, Trump's family, associates, and his proper-ties have been under electronic surveillance for years.[17] There is an enormous list of Trump employees that show up in in the "Project Dragnet" database. People running his golf courses, individuals in the Trump Organization, his ex-wife Ivana, and many others. An article by Infowars.com entitled:

"NSA DOCUMENTS PROVE SURVEILLANCE OF DONALD TRUMP & HIS FAMILY

Bombshell discovery shows targets of NSA's 'Project Dragnet' By Dr. Jerome Corsi, March 20, 2017. Here are a few excerpts from that article:

Electronic surveillance of Donald Trump was listed in the database for the following companies, locations, and dates:

Trump International
1 Central Park, NYC, NY
2008

Trump World Tower
845 United Nations Plaza, NYC, NY
No Date

Trump Tower SAL
108 Central Park, NYC, NY
2007

Trump Palace Co
200 E. 69th Street A, NYC, NY
2008

Trump Entertainment
725 Fifth Ave. FL, NYC, NY
2007

Trump Organization
725 Fifth Ave. BSM, NYC, NY
2009

Trump Palace
725 Fifth Ave., NYC, NY
2004

Mar-a-Lago Club
1100 S. Ocean BL, Palm Beach, FL
2006

Trump International
401 N. Wabash Ave., Chicago, IL
2008

Douglass Limousine
239 Nassau St., Princeton, NJ
2008

Trump International
3505 Summit BLV, West Palm Beach, FL
2004

Flights INC
P.O. Box 196, Hamilton MA
2004

Trump International
1 Central Park, NYC, NY
2008

Trump Hotels
Huron Ave., Atlantic City, NJ
No Date

Trump National
339 Pine Rd, Briarcliff, NY
No Date

Trump Plaza & C
2500 Pacific Ave, Atlantic City, NJ
2008

Trump Palace Co.
200 E. 69th St., NYC, NY
2008

Seven Springs
66 Oregon Rd, Mount Kisco, NY
2006-2008

The Project Dragnet database suggests Trump was under surveillance not only for phone conversations, but also for financial information, including most likely bank account transactions, credit card transactions, and tax filings.

Both federal and state law enforcement have had access to the Project Dragnet database, allowing widespread use for methods such as parallel construction. The practice, outlined in the 2013 Reuters article, "U.S. directs agents to cover up program used to investigate Americans," reveals the breadth of information that trickles down to law enforcement from high-level intelligence agencies."

Dr. Corsi broke another huge story recently. The Obama administration had a scheme to steal money from Fannie and Freddie mortgage companies. Hundreds of Billions of dollars were taken to fund the bankrupt Obamacare. This story has been confirmed by the new Treasury Secretary, Steven Mnuchin himself.[18]

Where's the outrage from Barack Obama over the assassination of Seth Rich, a former DNC staffer? There needs to be a federal investigation of this cold-blooded assassination. Donna Brazile needs to be publicly questioned on why she is warning off a private eye investigating this matter. This Seth Rich murder case is a big deal. What is the DNC hiding?

People like former CIA Director John Brennan, former Director of National Intelligence James Clapper, former CIA Director and NSA Director Michael Hayden, and Obama himself need to be dragged in front of both congressional investigations and Grand Juries, and they need to tell the American people what they knew and when they knew it. They think the American people are suckers. It's up to us to show them we're not, by exposing their corruption in front of the entire world.

Obama must also answer for putting that piece of garbage in the NDAA that put a 'Ministry of Truth' supervisory, governmental board over free speech in America. I've mentioned several times in this book how the **"Countering Disinformation And Propaganda Act"** was signed into law recently by Obama before he left. That's because it is so incredibly dangerous! Google banning hundreds of online publications![19] When will people wake the hell up? Who the fuck cares about football, dumb shows on television, and mindless cultural garbage. Look at what the establishment, deep state is doing!

Obama also needs to be held accountable for the fact that our nation's infrastructure is literally collapsing and is structurally deficient. It's dangerous just driving on American roads, bridges, highways, tunnels, and everything else.[20] There comes the point when government's gross negligence becomes so unbearable. When Obama neglects our infrastructure is that not making all of us less safe? Isn't that putting all our lives at risk? The answer is yes.

Obama needs to be held responsible for the heroes we lost at Benghazi.[21]

Obama needs to be held to account for the American Veterans who died because of incompetence at the Veterans Administration.[22]

Whether it's insulting the American people, leaving us open to attacks with WIDE OPEN BORDERS, promoting the elitists globalist agenda, doubling the debt, attempting to delegitimize President Trump, the IRS scandal, having zero respect for the Constitution, an infinite number of executive orders, taking money from Soros and people like Soros, spying on journalists, the attack on our heroes' lives in Benghazi, choosing Hillary Clinton as Secretary of State, Hillary's email scandal, the Iran deal giving billions to people who hate us and want us dead, the Veterans Administration scandals and failing our brave American heroes, Solyndra green energy scams, a justice department working against the people, Eric Holder in contempt of

Congress, dividing Americans racially, demonizing the police, illegal alien amnesty, constant power grabs, promoting cultural garbage and mindlessness, trading Taliban leaders for traitor Bergdahl, a steady appointment of "czars" to run agencies without Senate approval, illegally conducting a war against Libya helping further destabilize the region, ties to the Muslim Brotherhood, cutting off discussion about Obama's radical past, refusing to prosecute the new black panthers, hating freedom, hating American workers, setting us back years, calling Pennsylvanians bitter clingers, insulting the legacy of our founding fathers including George Washington, always lying, breaking promises, playing the people for suckers, or turning us into a laughing stock around the world Obama is the worst president in the history of the United States of America. He should be heavily prosecuted on every and all counts of wrongdoing. The law must apply to everyone. It can't just apply to the average person trying to live the American dream, and not apply to tyrants like Barack Hussein Obama II.

Fifteen

AMERICA'S WAY FORWARD

America is under vicious attack. It's not a conspiracy theory. Globalists in the United States and around the world publicly hate our nation and want us destroyed. It's about money and control. If the United States of America goes belly up, it's more profitable for them, and they can more efficiently manage our population. They fundamentally hate freedom and competition. That's why America's sovereignty is under attack. This is why our economy is under attack. This is why we're under attack culturally, spiritually, and educationally. It's why our jobs have been shipped overseas. It's why tens of millions of our fellow Americans live in poverty. It's why so many people are struggling to make ends meet. It's why so many people feel like the American dream is unachievable. It's why so many Americans feel hopeless. Many spineless politicians, including both democrats and republicans, not only refuse to stand up for us, they accept money from a known Nazi collaborator, George Soros. Think about that for a minute. They have investigations right now in Congress about "Russian interference" which is about deflecting away from the real criminality going on in our government. I have a better idea, how about we have a Nazi investigation. Let's have Congress investigate the ties and connections of establishment politicians who take money from Soros. Let's investigate all the real illegality, fraud, abuse, and traitorous activity that has gone on. Construction of the border wall has not yet begun, but hopefully, it will soon. Democrats and even some Republicans will oppose this. Why? Because they are against our very existence. Our right to exist as a Country. That's what globalism is. It's about you having no right whatsoever to even exist. Globalism is about making you feel sad, depressed, alone, economically weak, physically weak, mentally weak, spiritually bankrupt, sick, and surrounded by cultural garbage and nonsense. They write public documents explaining their desire to limit human population and make us sterile.

Meanwhile, American men are really concerned about what goes on in the NFL. Being a man is about having the courage to stand up to the politically correct fools, the authoritarian left, the fake conservative elements of the Republican establishment, the neocons who want constant war, the globalists who try dissolve our country's sovereignty, the weak/selfish/incompetent politicians getting us further in debt, tyrants like Obama who pass laws to limit your free speech, central banks ripping off the American people, propaganda media causing divisiveness, radical Islam, communists marching on our streets with flags that have the hammer and sickle, China hurting us economically, Washington lobbyists who put their own interests before the American peoples' interests, big corporate monopolies, disconnected elites, criminal cartels bringing drugs into America, illegal aliens raping and killing innocent people, and arrogant Ivy League professors who lie to their students. It's not about distractions like the NFL. We need priorities right now. A few days ago, a cowardly terrorist loser shot multiple people at a Republican congressional baseball practice, including Congressman Steve Scalise, who is a part of U.S. House leadership. The terrorist asked if it was republicans or democrats practicing on the field. He found out it was Republicans and started shooting shortly after. The Capitol Police showed extraordinary bravery in stopping the terrorist, and they deserve recognition for that. Congressman Scalise is still recovering, and we should pray for him, his family, and all the victims of this attack.

America needs to wake up and realize the gravity of the situation we face. If the American people ever fully awakened, we could be unstoppable. It is possible to have a better economy, better infrastructure, revive the American dream, have better healthcare, have real competition in every aspect of our economy which will create lower prices/ better quality, have more unity and less division, bring God back, bring freedom back, bring the constitution back, appreciate nature, better education, better trade deals, more peace, more civil liberties, legal immigration, less taxes, less regulation, less government surveillance, and more dreams, hope, excitement, and optimism about the future. I know it can be tremendously depressing to think about all the enemies America has around the world. It can be exceptionally heartbreaking to think about all the activity of the globalists. The darkness of globalism is very real, and it's incredibly powerful. There is good news, though. Globalism can and is being defeated. Many Americans are waking up. President Trump understands these threats, and that helps tremendously because it forces the discussion of these important topics. Other countries around the world are also waking up. The darkness of globalism, like any darkness, is defeated with light. That light comes from common sense, freedom, honor, optimism, courage, physical and mental strength, mental clarity, understanding who we are, our dreams and aspirations, conquering the fear, letting God back into our hearts, caring about our fellow Americans, having humility, draining the swamp in Washington D.C., putting our destinies back in our own hands, and becoming America again. We can make America Great Again, and more importantly, we can Make It Greater than Ever Before. Acknowledge God and the real power of this Universe, that the enemies want to disconnect you from. We need to value qualities like intelligence, patriotism, order, originality, practicality, strength, success, thankfulness, calmness, freedom, grace, clear mindedness, love, loyalty, trustworthiness, uniqueness, vitality, enjoyment, prudence, adventurousness, ambition, compassion, co-operation, determination, diligence, elegance, enthusiasm, openness, justice, curiosity, inner harmony, focus, independence, and happiness.

It begins with us becoming America again. President Trump said "There is no such thing as a global anthem, a global currency, or a global flag. This is the United States of America that I am representing. I am not representing the globe. I am representing your country."[1] He's exactly right. There is nothing wrong with putting American first. There is nothing wrong about striving for real American exceptionalism. That doesn't mean we can go around the world and do whatever we want, but we can and should be proud of our Country and our values. Once we become America again, we can start focusing on achieving our dreams. Gail Devers is an American track and field star, an Olympic champion, and an incredible woman. She beat Grave's disease, an immune system, and thyroid disorder, and even had to undergo radiation treatment. She went on to win multiple Olympic gold medals in 1992 and 1996.[2] An incredible story. Gail Devers said that to "Keep your dreams alive. Understand to achieve anything requires faith and belief in yourself, vision, hard work, determination, and dedication. Remember all things are possible for those who believe."[3] And she's exactly right, we must keep our dreams alive. Recently, President Trump gave a state of the union speech that was the best I've ever seen in my life.[4] It was phenomenal. My favorite part was when he said:

"The time for small thinking is over. The time for trivial fights is behind us.

We just need the courage to share the dreams that fill our hearts.

The bravery to express the hopes that stir our souls.

And the confidence to turn those hopes and dreams to action.

From now on, America will be empowered by our aspirations, not burdened by our fears inspired by the future, not bound by the failures of the past and guided by our vision, not blinded by our doubts.

I am asking all citizens to embrace this Renewal of the American Spirit. I am asking all members of Congress to join me in dreaming big, and bold and daring things for our country. And I am asking everyone watching tonight to seize this moment and Believe in yourselves.

Believe in your future.

And believe, once more, in America."

Amazing. Empowered by our aspirations, not burdened by our fears. That's what America is about.

One of the ways we overcome those fears and achieve our dreams and success is by becoming the best versions of ourselves that we can be. Working to be the best we can from a physical, mental, and spiritual standpoint.

Be your best Physically. Eat vitamins. Exercise. Check out inforwars.com/store all natural health products. Eat healthy foods. Be proactive in making your body as healthy and vigorous as possible.

Be your best Mentally. Read books. Follow up on what's going on politically. Study history. Read. Learn. Study. Expand your vocabulary. Strive for mental focus and clarity. Take vitamins that help with memory. Understand you'll never be able to reach the full potential of your brain. Be as smart as you humanly can.

Be your best spiritually. I'm a Christian, and I believe in God. Care about others. Don't be a predator who wants to take advantage of uninformed people. We have to educate them. Let's care about our fellow citizens who are struggling. If you're not religious, just try your best to be a great person. Have compassion. Have a big heart. Value freedom. Be honorable. Stand up for what's right. Have faith in what is possible.

We can and will defeat globalism. We don't need to be intimidated by George Soros. We don't have to be intimidated by tyrants like Obama. We don't need to be intimidated by leftist, authoritarian language/thought/political/cultural police. We don't have to be intimidated by rogue, criminal, deep state elements of society that undermine our civil liberties. The Darkness of Globalism is defeated by a light that is infinitely stronger and more powerful. The darkness of globalism is defeated by God, it's defeated by honor, it's defeated by courage, it's defeated by intelligence, it's defeated by inner strength, it's defeated by our aspirations and our dreams, it's defeated through freedom, it's defeated through success, it's defeated by exuberance, it's defeated by Love.

A Tribute to Patriots

President Donald J Trump
First Lady Melania Trump
Vice President Mike Pence
Alex Jones
Roger Stone
Wayne Allyn Root
Stephen Bannon
Matt Drudge
Paul Joseph Watson
Dr. Jerome Corsi
Sean Hannity
Congressman Steve Scalise
Mark Levin
Michael Savage
Stefan Molyneux
William Binney
Laura Ingraham
Ann Coulter
Sheriff David Clarke
Mike Huckabee
Sarah Palin
Kellyanne Conway
Mark Dice
Mike Cernovich
James O'Keefe
Milo Yiannopoulos
Lynnette Hardaway and Rochelle Richardson aka
"Diamond and Silk"
Jack Posobiec
And millions more…

Powerful Quotes

"Only a virtuous people are capable of freedom. As nations become corrupt and vicious, they have more need of masters."

—BENJAMIN FRANKLIN

"America is too great for small dreams."

—PRESIDENT RONALD REAGAN

"Freedom is one of the deepest and noblest aspirations of the human spirit."

—PRESIDENT RONALD REAGAN

"We are never defeated unless we give up on God."

—PRESIDENT RONALD REAGAN

"I like the dreams of the future better than the history of the past."

—THOMAS JEFFERSON

"We hold these truths to be self—evident: that all men are created equal; that they are endowed by their Creator with certain unalienable rights; that among these are life, liberty, and the pursuit of happiness."

—THOMAS JEFFERSON

"Educate and inform the whole mass of the people... They are the only sure reliance for the preservation of our liberty."

—THOMAS JEFFERSON

"The life of the nation is secure only while the nation is honest, truthful, and virtuous."

—FREDERICK DOUGLASS

"The limits of tyrants are prescribed by the endurance of those whom they oppress."

—FREDERICK DOUGLASS

"If the freedom of speech is taken away then dumb and silent we may be led, like sheep to the slaughter."

—GEORGE WASHINGTON

*"Liberty, when it begins to take root,
is a plant of rapid growth."*

—George Washington

*"The Constitution is the guide which
I never will abandon."*

—George Washington

*"Keep your eyes on the stars, and
your feet on the ground."*

—Theodore Roosevelt

*"Love is the only force capable of
transforming an enemy into a friend."*

—MLK

*"The function of education is to teach one to think
intensively and to think critically. Intelligence plus
character — that is the goal of true education."*

—MLK

*"Nothing in all the world is more dangerous than
sincere ignorance and conscientious stupidity."*

—MLK

*"Our lives begin to end the day we become
silent about things that matter."*

—MLK

*"Darkness cannot drive out darkness;
only light can do that. Hate cannot drive
out hate; only love can do that."*

—MLK

*"False words are not only evil in themselves,
but they infect the soul with evil."*

—Socrates

*"Accept the challenges so that you can
feel the exhilaration of victory."*

—General George Patton

*"Success consists of going from failure to
failure without loss of enthusiasm."*

—WINSTON CHURCHILL

"Never, never, never give up."

—WINSTON CHURCHILL

*"Every violation of truth is not only a sort of suicide in
the liar, but is a stab at the health of human society."*

—RALPH WALDO EMERSON

*"Do not let your hearts be troubled.
Trust in God; trust also in me."*

—JESUS CHRIST

*"For what shall it profit a man, if he gain the
whole world, and suffer the loss of his soul?"*

—JESUS CHRIST

"America will never be destroyed from the outside. If we falter and lose our freedoms, it will be because we destroyed ourselves."

—ABRAHAM LINCOLN

Notes

Introduction

1. "Somebody Invested in Roads and Bridges ... You Didn't Build That." *C-SPAN*. N.p., 13 July 2012. Web. 14 Mar. 2017. <https://www.c-span.org/video/?c4568668/somebody-invested-roads-bridges-didnt-build>.

2. Durden, Tyler. "Obama Quietly Signs The "Countering Disinformation And Propaganda Act" Into Law." *ZeroHedge*. N.p., 26 Dec. 2016. Web. 15 Jan. 2017. <http://www.zerohedge.com/news/2016-12-24/obama-signs-countering-disinformation-and-propaganda-act-law>.

3. "All Info - H.R.5181 - 114th Congress (2015-2016): Countering Foreign Propaganda and Disinformation Act of 2016." *Congress.gov*. N.p., 10 May 2016. Web. 15 Jan. 2017. <https://www.congress.gov/bill/114th-congress/house-bill/5181/all-info>.

4. Kerr, Andrew. "The Nuts and Bolts of the "Countering Disinformation And Propaganda Act"."*The Citizens Audit*. N.p., 28 Dec. 2016. Web. 9 Feb. 2017. <http://www.thecitizensaudit.com/2016/12/28/the-nuts-and-bolts-of-the-countering-disinformation-and-propaganda-act/>.

5. "8 Vicious Attacks On Trump Supporters - Tea Party News." *Tea Party*. N.p., 18 Nov. 2016. Web. 18 Feb. 2017. <https://www.teaparty.org/8-vicious-attacks-trump-supporters-200932/>.

Nationalism vs Globalism

1. Wilde, Robert. "The History of the European Union (EU)." *ThoughtCo.* N.p., 25 Mar. 2017. Web. 29 Mar. 2017. <https://www.thoughtco.com/the-history-of-the-european-union-1221595>.

2. Gabel, Matthew J. "European Union (EU)." *Encyclopædia Britannica.* Encyclopædia Britannica, Inc., 24 June 2016. Web. 27 Feb. 2017. <https://www.britannica.com/topic/European-Union>.

3. Fjordman. "Ten Reasons to Get Rid of the European Union." *Europe News.* N.p., 12 Oct. 2008. Web. 21 Jan. 2017. <https://en.europenews.dk/Ten-Reasons-to-Get-Rid-of-the-European-Union-78453.html>.

4. The Editors of Encyclopædia Britannica. "Renaissance." *Encyclopædia Britannica.* Encyclopædia Britannica, Inc., 02 May 2017. Web. 4 May 2017. <https://www.britannica.com/event/Renaissance>.

5. Szalay, Jessie. "The Renaissance: The 'Rebirth' of Science & Culture." *LiveScience.* Purch, 29 June 2016. Web. 15 Feb. 2017. <https://www.livescience.com/55230-renaissance.html>.

6. History.com Staff. "Renaissance Art." *History.com.* A&E Television Networks, 2010. Web. 4 Feb. 2017. <http://www.history.com/topics/renaissance-art>.

7. Ernst, Douglas. "Sean Hannity Does Victory Lap after Donald Trump Victory: 'Get Juan Williams off That Ledge'." *The Washington Times.* The Washington Times, 09 Nov. 2016. Web.

21 Jan. 2017. <http://m.washingtontimes.com/news/2016/nov/9/ sean-hannity-does-victory-lap-after-donald-trump-v/>.

Soros

1. "Martin Luther King, Jr. Quotes." *BrainyQuote*. Xplore, n.d. Web. 19 Jan. 2017. <https://www.brainyquote.com/quotes/quotes/m/ martinluth124474.html>.

2. "Albert Einstein Quotes." *BrainyQuote*. Xplore, n.d. Web. 19 Feb. 2017. <https://www.brainyquote.com/quotes/quotes/a/alber-teins143096.html>.

3. "Winston Churchill Quotes." *BrainyQuote*. Xplore, n.d. Web. 19 Feb. 2017. <https://www.brainyquote.com/quotes/authors/w/ winston_churchill.html>.

4. Posted by JoeConservative. "1998 "60 Minutes Interview" of Evil "Guiltless" Soros Uncovered!" *IPatriot*. N.p., 15 Nov. 2016. Web. 20 Feb. 2017. <http://ipatriot.com/1998-60-minutes-interview-evil-atheist-soros-uncovered/>.

5. Ehrenfeld, Rachel, and Shawn Macomber. "George Soros: The 'God' Who Carries Around Some Dangerous Demons." *Los Angeles Times*. Los Angeles Times, 04 Oct. 2004. Web. 11 Feb. 2017. <http://articles.latimes.com/2004/oct/04/opinion/ oe-ehrenfeld4>.

6. Nash, Charlie. "'Refuse Fascism' Group Behind Berkeley Riot Received $50k from George Soros." *Breitbart*. N.p., 05 Feb. 2017.

Web. 18 Mar. 2017. <http://www.breitbart.com/milo/2017/02/05/refuse-fascism-group-behind-berkeley-riot-funded-george-soros/>.

7. Samuelson, D. "The Disturbing History of George Soros That Every American Should Know." *Newstarget.com*. N.p., 28 Nov. 2016. Web. 22 Jan. 2017. <http://www.newstarget.com/2016-11-28-the-disturbing-history-of-george-soros-that-every-american-should-know.html>.

8. Morris, M. "10 Dark Secrets Of George Soros." *Listverse*. N.p., 21 Oct. 2016. Web. 5 Feb. 2017. <http://listverse.com/2016/10/21/10-dark-secrets-of-george-soros/>.

9. Boyer, Mike. "Soros Buys Halliburton." *Foreign Policy*. N.p., 27 Feb. 2007. Web. 23 Jan. 2017. <http://foreignpolicy.com/2007/02/27/soros-buys-halliburton/>.

10. Slad. "Destroying America Will Be the Culmination of My Life's Work. George Soros." *Republic Broadcasting Network*. N.p., 28 Apr. 2016. Web. 19 Feb. 2017. <https://republicbroadcasting.org/news/destroying-america-will-be-the-culmination-of-my-lifes-work-george-soros/>.

11. Dennin, Mike. "George Soros Quotes on Government: 10 Memorable Statements From Billionaire." *Newsmax*. N.p., 02 Nov. 2015. Web. 13 Feb. 2017. <http://www.newsmax.com/FastFeatures/george-soros-quotes-government/2015/11/02/id/700216/>.

12. Farah, Joseph. "A Novel Idea: Revoke George Soros' Citizenship." *WND*. N.p., 9 Feb. 2017. Web. 3 Mar. 2017. <http://www.wnd.com/2017/02/a-novel-idea-revoke-george-soros-citizenship/>.

13. Klein, Aaron. "Soros-Funded Media Matters Secretly Plotting to 'Stop' Breitbart News."*Breitbart*. N.p., 27 Jan. 2017. Web. 15 Feb. 2017. <http://www.breitbart.com/big-journalism/2017/01/27/soros-funded-media-matters-secretly-plotting-stop-breitbart-news/>.

14. Corsi, Jerome R. "Leaked Docs: Media Matters Conspires with Facebook, Google to Shut down Conservative Media." *Intellihub*. N.p., 08 Feb. 2017. Web. 14 Mar. 2017. <https://www.intelli-hub.com/leaked-docs-media-matters-conspires-with-facebook-google-to-shut-down-conservative-media/>.

15. Shroyer, Owen, and Andrew Kerr. "Media Matters Tax Fraud Exposed." *Infowars*. N.p., 30 Sept. 2016. Web. 9 Feb. 2017. <https://www.infowars.com/media-matters-tax-fraud-exposed/>.

16. Zuckerman, Gregory, and Juliet Chung. "Billionaire George Soros Lost Nearly $1 Billion in Weeks After Trump Election." *The Wall Street Journal*. Dow Jones & Company, 13 Jan. 2017. Web. 9 Feb. 2017. <https://www.wsj.com/articles/billionaire-george-soros-lost-nearly-1-billion-in-weeks-after-trump-election-1484227167>.

17. Lucas, Fred. "Soros Fingerprints All Over Anti-Trump Lawsuits." *LifeZette*. N.p., 06 Feb. 2017. Web. 19 Feb. 2017. <http://www.lifezette.com/polizette/soros-fingerprints-all-over-anti-trump-lawsuits/>.

18. Cox, Jeff. "George Soros Calls Trump a 'would-be Dictator' Who 'is Going to Fail'." *CNBC*. CNBC, 19 Jan. 2017. Web. 20 Feb. 2017. <http://www.cnbc.com/2017/01/19/george-soros-calls-donald-trump-a-would-be-dictator-who-is-going-to-fail.html>.

19. Klein, Aaron. "Obama's Organizing for Action Partners with Soros-Linked 'Indivisible' to Disrupt Trump's Agenda." *Breitbart.* N.p., 19 Feb. 2017. Web. 12 Mar. 2017. <http://www.breitbart. com/big-government/2017/02/19/obamas-organizing-action-partners-soros-linked-indivisible-disrupt-trumps-agenda/>.

Dangerous Foundations

1. Maessen, Jurriaan. "For The Record: Rockefeller Soft Kill Depopulation Plans Exposed."*Infowars.* N.p., 26 Mar. 2012. Web. 17 Feb. 2017. <https://www.infowars.com/for-the-record -rockefeller-soft-kill-depopulation-plans-exposed/>.

2. "Annual Reports." *The Rockefeller Foundation.* The Rockefeller Foundation, n.d. Web. 9 Feb. 2017. <https://www.rockefeller-foundation.org/about-us/governance-reports/annual-reports/>.

3. Gordon, Deborah. "What the World Needs Now Is Climate-Conscious Cohorts." *Carnegie Endowment for International Peace.* N.p., 21 Dec. 2016. Web. 15 Feb. 2017. <http://carnegieendow-ment.org/2016/12/21/what-world-needs-now-is-climate-con-scious-cohorts-pub-66536>.

Propaganda Media

1. Nolan, Lucas. "6 Reasons Why ABC News Is Unqualified to Label 'Fake News'." *Breitbart.* N.p., 22 Dec. 2016. Web. 18 Mar. 2017. <http://www.breitbart.com/tech/2016/12/22/6-reasons-why-abc-news-is-unqualified-to-label-fake-news/>.

2. Rahn, Will. "Commentary: The Unbearable Smugness of the Press." *CBS News*. CBS Interactive, 10 Nov. 2016. Web. 13 Feb. 2017. <http://www.cbsnews.com/news/commentary-the-unbearable-smugness-of-the-press-presidential-election-2016/>.

3. Pollak, Joel B. "5 Times Lester Holt Shilled for Hillary Clinton at First Debate." *Breitbart*. N.p., 26 Sept. 2016. Web. 27 Jan. 2017. <http://www.breitbart.com/big-government/2016/09/26/lester-holt-candy-crowley-moment-first-debate/>.

4. "Truth, War Propaganda, CIA and Media Manipulation." *Global Research*. N.p., 31 Mar. 2011. Web. 16 Mar. 2017. <http://www.globalresearch.ca/truth-propaganda-and-media-manipulation/23868>.

5. "New Email Shows DNC Boss Giving Clinton Camp Debate Question in Advance." *Fox News*. FOX News Network, 31 Oct. 2016. Web. 15 Feb. 2017. <http://www.foxnews.com/politics/2016/10/31/new-email-shows-dnc-boss-giving-clinton-camp-debate-question-in-advance.html>.

6. Jones, Susan. "Donna Brazile Tells Campaign That Hillary Will Get a Debate Question 'From a Woman With a Rash'." *CNS News*. N.p., 31 Oct. 2016. Web. 20 Feb. 2017. <http://www.cnsnews.com/news/article/susan-jones/donna-brazile-tells-campaign-hillary-will-get-debate-question-woman-rash>.

7. Kant, Garth. "Trump Fallout: Major Media Admit Liberal Bias." *WND*. N.p., 10 Nov. 2016. Web. 18 Feb. 2017. <http://www.wnd.com/2016/11/trump-fallout-major-media-admit-liberal-bias/>.

8. Rutenberg, Jim. "A 'Dewey Defeats Truman' Lesson for the Digital Age." *The New York Times*. The New York Times, 09 Nov. 2016. Web. 19 Feb. 2017. <https://www.nytimes.com/2016/11/09/business/media/media-trump-clinton.html?mcubz=1>.

9. Munro, Neil. "ACLU Backs Zuckerberg Censorship of New Media on Facebook." *Breitbart*. N.p., 16 Dec. 2016. Web. 1 Mar. 2017. <http://www.breitbart.com/big-government/2016/12/16/facebook-aclu-fake-news/>.

10. Durden, Tyler. "Google Permanently Bans 200 "Fake News" Sites." *ZeroHedge*. N.p., 25 Jan. 2017. Web. 20 Feb. 2017. <http://www.zerohedge.com/news/2017-01-25/google-permanently-bans-200-fake-news-sites>.

CIA

1. Pike, John, and Steven Aftergood. "HISTORY." *CIA - History*. N.p., 23 Sept. 1996. Web. 2 Mar. 2017. <https://fas.org/irp/cia/ciahist.htm>.

2. "History of the CIA." *Central Intelligence Agency*. Central Intelligence Agency, 18 Feb. 2014. Web. 4 Feb. 2017. <https://www.cia.gov/about-cia/history-of-the-cia>.

3. Louise, Mary. "Operation Mockingbird: CIA Media Manipulation." *OPERATION MOCKINGBIRD Part 1*. AMERICAN PATRIOT FRIENDS NETWORK, n.d. Web. 8 Mar. 2017. <http://www.apfn.org/apfn/mockingbird.htm>.

4. Kangas, Steve, and William Blum. "A Timeline of CIA Atrocities." N.p., 17 May 2016. Web. 8 Mar. 2017. <http://www.globalre-search.ca/a-timeline-of-cia-atrocities/5348804>.

5. U.S. Senate. "Church Committee: Book II - Intelligence Activities and the Rights of Americans." N.p., 26 Apr. 1976. Web. 20 Mar. 2017. <https://www.maryferrell.org/showDoc.html?docId=1158#relPageId=1&tab=page>.

6. U.S. Senate. "Church Committee: Book V - The Investigation of the Assassination of President John F. Kennedy: Performance of the Intelligence Agencies." N.p., 23 Apr. 1976. Web. 20 Mar. 2017. <https://www.maryferrell.org/showDoc.html?docId=1161#relPageId=29&tab=page>.

China

1. Sipra, Afzal. *Point2ponder.com*. N.p., 26 Dec. 2016. Web. 17 Feb. 2017. <http://point2ponder.com/evolution-also-kind-revolution/>.

2. "Mao Tse-Tung." *Iz Quotes*. N.p., n.d. Web. 23 Feb. 2017. <http://izquotes.com/quote/392984>.

3. History.com Staff. "Mao Zedong." *History.com*. A&E Television Networks, 2009. Web. 19 Apr. 2017. <http://www.history.com/topics/cold-war/mao-zedong>.

4. "Mao Zedong Quotes." *BrainyQuote*. Xplore, n.d. Web. 3 Mar. 2017. <https://www.brainyquote.com/quotes/authors/m/mao_zedong.html>.

5. Denyer, Simon. "China's Scary Lesson to the World: Censoring the Internet Works." *The Washington Post.* WP Company, 23 May 2016. Web. 15 Mar. 2017. <https://www.washingtonpost.com/world/asia_pacific/chinas-scary-lesson-to-the-world-censoring-the-internet-works/2016/05/23/413afe78-fff3-11e5-8bb1-f124a43f84dc_story.html>.

6. Jacobs, Sarah. "29 Eerie Photos That Show Just How Polluted China's Air Has Become."*Business Insider.* Business Insider, 05 Jan. 2017. Web. 14 Mar. 2017. <http://www.businessinsider.com/eerie-photos-of-air-pollution-in-china-2017-1>.

7. News. "South China Sea Artificial Islands Have Weapons Installed: Report." *NBCNews.com.* NBCUniversal News Group, 15 Dec. 2016. Web. 23 Feb. 2017. <http://www.nbcnews.com/news/china/south-china-sea-artificial-islands-have-weapons-installed-report-n696311>.

8. Riley, Charles. "China's Richest Man Still Wants to Buy a Hollywood Studio." *CNNMoney.* Cable News Network, 18 Jan. 2017. Web. 5 Mar. 2017. <http://money.cnn.com/2017/01/18/media/wang-jianlin-hollywood-studio-davos/index.html?iid=EL>.

9. WSJVideo. "China's Xi Jinping Issues a Defense of Globalization." *The Wall Street Journal.* Dow Jones & Company, 17 Jan. 2017. Web. 7 Apr. 2017. <http://www.wsj.com/video/china-xi-jinping-issues-a-defense-of-globalization/ED9C1221-B763-419B-8F93-A488A67A7D8C.html>.

Hollywood

1. Bacharach, Elizabeth. "37 Celebrities Who Have All Slammed Donald Trump."*Cosmopolitan*. Cosmopolitan, 20 Oct. 2016. Web. 17 Feb. 2017. <http://www.cosmopolitan.com/politics/a6129330/celebrities-react-hate-tweets-donald-trump/>.

2. Posted By Ian Schwartz. "Will Smith: "Cleanse" Trump Supporters Out Of Our Country."*Video RealClearPolitics*. N.p., 9 Aug. 2016. Web. 19 Feb. 2017. <https://www.realclearpolitics.com/video/2016/08/09/will_smith_cleanse_trump_supporters_out_of_our_country.html>.

3. Chen, Joyce. "J.Law: Donald Trump Becoming President Would "Be the End of the World"."*Us Weekly*. Us Weekly, 01 Oct. 2015. Web. 17 Feb. 2017. <http://www.usmagazine.com/celebrity-news/news/jennifer-lawrence-president-donald-trump-would-be-end-of-the-world-2015110>.

4. Pulver, Andrew. "George Clooney Interview: 'Donald Trump Is a Xenophobic Fascist'." *The Guardian*. Guardian News and Media, 03 Mar. 2016. Web. 7 Mar. 2017. <https://www.theguardian.com/film/2016/mar/03/george-clooney-donald-trump-is-a-xenophobic-fascist>.

5. Hayden, Erik. "Why Jennifer Holliday Decided Against Performing at Trump's Inauguration (Q&A)." *The Hollywood Reporter*. N.p., 14 Jan. 2017. Web. 17 Feb. 2017. <http://www.hollywoodreporter.com/news/why-jennifer-holliday-decided-performing-at-trumps-inauguration-q-a-964377>.

6. Nolte, John. "New Hollywood Blacklist: Oppose Trump or Face Career Ruin, Racism, Sexism, Threats." *Daily Wire*. N.p., 17 Jan. 2017. Web. 13 Mar. 2017. <http://www.dailywire.com/news/12479/new-hollywood-blacklist-oppose-trump-or-face-john-nolte>.

7. "Quotes About Hollywood (170 Quotes)." *(170 Quotes)*. Goodreads.com, n.d. Web. 19 Feb. 2017. <http://www.goodreads.com/quotes/tag/hollywood>.

United Nations

1. History.com Staff. "The United Nations Is Born." *History.com*. A&E Television Networks, 2009. Web. 5 May 2017. <http://www.history.com/this-day-in-history/the-united-nations-is-born>.

2. Newman, Alex. "Amid Tsunami of Scandals, UN Ignores Massive Corruption." *The New American*. N.p., 25 July 2016. Web. 20 Feb. 2017. <https://www.thenewamerican.com/world-news/europe/item/23708-amid-tsunami-of-scandals-un-ignores-massive-corruption>.

3. McCoy, Kevin. "Six Charged in Alleged U.N. Corruption Scheme." *USA Today*. Gannett Satellite Information Network, 06 Oct. 2015. Web. 15 Mar. 2017. <https://www.usatoday.com/story/money/2015/10/06/united-nations-bribe-scheme-busted/73438750/>.

4. Banbury, Anthony. "I Love the U.N., but It Is Failing." *The New York Times*. The New York Times, 18 Mar. 2016. Web. 9 Feb. 2017. <https://www.nytimes.com/2016/03/20/opinion/sunday/i-love-the-un-but-it-is-failing.html?mcubz=1>.

5. Bartsiotas, George A., and Gopinathan Achamkulangare. "FRAUD PREVENTION, DETECTION AND RESPONSE IN UNITED NATIONS SYSTEM ORGANIZATIONS." *Joint Inspection Unit.* United Nations, Geneva, 2016. Web. 17 Mar. 2017. <https://www.unjiu.org/en/reports-notes/JIU%20Products/JIU_REP_2016_4_English.pdf>.

6. Charbonneau, Louis, Michelle Nichols, and Nate Raymond. "Exclusive: U.N. Audit Identifies Serious Lapses Linked to Alleged Bribery." *Reuters.* N.p., 03 Apr. 2016. Web. 1 Apr. 2017. <http://www.reuters.com/article/us-un-corruption-exclusive-idUSKCN0X00VD>.

7. "United Nations Conference on Environment and Development AGENDA 21." (n.d.): n. pag. June 1992. Web. 20 Mar. 2017. <https://sustainabledevelopment.un.org/content/documents/Agenda21.pdf>.

Academia

1. Rodman, Melissa C., Luca F. Schroeder, and Idrees M. Kahloon. "Faculty Overwhelmingly Donate to Clinton | News | The Harvard Crimson." *Harvard News.* The Crimson, 10 Feb. 2016. Web. 17 Mar. 2017. <http://www.thecrimson.com/article/2016/2/10/faculty-donate-clinton-2016/>.

2. Talasani, Vishal. "Employees of Elite Universities Donate to Clinton Over Trump by Wide Margins." *The Chicago Maroon.* The Chicago Maroon, 4 Nov. 2016. Web. 15 Apr. 2017. <https://www.chicagomaroon.com/article/2016/11/4/faculty-elite-institutions-donated-overwhelmingly/>.

3. Hoft, Jim. "Professor Spams His Students to Support Crooked Hillary, Then Blames It On Hackers." *The Gateway Pundit*. N.p., 09 Sept. 2016. Web. 9 Apr. 2017. <http://www.thegatewaypundit.com/2016/09/professor-spams-students-support-crooked-hillary-blames-hackers/>.

4. Piven, Frances Fox, and Richard Cloward. "The Weight of the Poor: A Strategy to End Poverty." *The Nation*. N.p., 20 July 2015. Web. 10 Mar. 2017. <https://www.thenation.com/article/weight-poor-strategy-end-poverty/>.

5. Kutner, Max. "IVY LEAGUERS WANT THEIR CAMPUSES TO BE 'SANCTUARIES' FROM TRUMP DEPORTATIONS." *Newsweek*. N.p., 14 Nov. 2016. Web. 10 May 2017. <http://www.newsweek.com/brown-university-sanctuary-deportation-trump-521075>.

6. Berman, Jillian. "Watch America's Student-loan Debt Grow $2,726 Every Second."*MarketWatch*. N.p., 30 Jan. 2016. Web. 14 Mar. 2017. <http://www.marketwatch.com/story/every-second-americans-get-buried-under-another-3055-in-student-loan-debt-2015-06-10>.

7. Park, Madison, and Kyung Lah. "Berkeley Protests of Yiannopoulos Caused $100,000 in Damage." *CNN*. Cable News Network, 02 Feb. 2017. Web. 9 Apr. 2017. <http://www.cnn.com/2017/02/01/us/milo-yiannopoulos-berkeley/index.html>.

Venezuela

1. Martel, Frances. "'Maduro Diet': 3 Out of 4 Venezuelans Lost 'At Least 19 Pounds' in 2016." *Breitbart*. N.p., 20 Feb. 2017. Web. 21 Mar. 2017. <http://www.breitbart.com/national-security/2017/02/20/maduro-diet-3-4-venezuelans-lost-19-pounds-2016/>.

2. "Study: Venezuelans Lost 19 Lbs. on Average over past Year Due to Lack of Food." *Fox News*. FOX News Network, 20 Feb. 2017. Web. 15 Mar. 2017. <http://www.foxnews.com/world/2017/02/20/study-venezuelans-lost-19-lb-on-average-over-past-year-due-to-lack-food.html>.

Central Banks

1. "Monetarists Anonymous." *The Economist*. The Economist Newspaper, 29 Sept. 2012. Web. 16 Mar. 2017. <http://www.economist.com/node/21563752>.

2. "Henry Ford Quotes." *BrainyQuote*. Xplore, n.d. Web. 17 Mar. 2017. <https://www.brainyquote.com/quotes/quotes/h/henry-ford136294.html>.

3. "Quotes from International Bankers and Fathers of America." *Rapidtrends.com*. N.p., n.d. Web. 19 Mar. 2017. <http://www.rapidtrends.com/quotes-from-international-bankers-and-fathers-of-america/>.

4. "Famous Quotations on Banking." *The Money Masters*. N.p., n.d. Web. 18 Mar. 2017. <http://www.themoneymasters.com/the-money-masters/famous-quotations-on-banking/>.

5. "Benjamin Franklin Quote." *A-Z Quotes*. N.p., n.d. Web. 19 Mar. 2017. <http://www.azquotes.com/quote/650867>.

6. Board of Governors of the Federal Reserve System. "Nelson W. Aldrich." *Federal Reserve History*. N.p., n.d. Web. 9 Apr. 2017. <https://www.federalreservehistory.org/people/nelson_w_aldrich>.

7. "Home." *Home | Federal Reserve History*. N.p., n.d. Web. 5 Feb. 2017. <http://www.federalreservehistory.org/>.

8. "Louis Thomas McFadden Quote." *A-Z Quotes*. N.p., n.d. Web. 15 Mar. 2017. <http://www.azquotes.com/quote/679668>.

9. *Quotations from the Documentary The Money Masters How Banks Create the World's Money*. N.p., n.d. Web. 17 Mar. 2017. <http://www.thirdworldtraveler.com/Banks/Money_Masters_quotations.html>.

10. "Charles A. Lindbergh." *Our Republic*. N.p., n.d. Web. 14 Mar. 2017. <http://www.ourrepubliconline.com/Author/112>.

11. "Louis McFadden Quotes/Quotations from Liberty Quotes." *LibertyQuotes*. N.p., n.d. Web. 11 Mar. 2017. <http://quotes.liberty-tree.ca/quotes_by/louis+mcfadden>.

12. History.com Staff. "FDR Takes United States off Gold Standard." *History.com*. A&E Television Networks, 2009. Web. 13 Apr. 2017. <http://www.history.com/this-day-in-history/fdr-takes-united-states-off-gold-standard>.

13. "Tasks." *European Central Bank*. Eurosystem, n.d. Web. 13 Mar. 2017. <https://www.ecb.europa.eu/ecb/tasks/html/index.en.html>.

14. *About the IMF*. International Monetary Fund, n.d. Web. 19 Mar. 2017. <http://www.imf.org/en/About>.

15. "WORLD TRADE ORGANIZATION." World Trade Organization, n.d. Web. 7 Mar. 2017. <https://www.wto.org/english/thewto_e/whatis_e/whatis_e.htm>.

16. "World Bank and IMF Are Established." *History Channel*. N.p., n.d. Web. 12 Mar. 2017. <http://www.historychannel.com.au/this-day-in-history/world-bank-and-imf-are-established/>.

17. Sjolin, Sara. "Why Goldman Sachs Staff Can Donate to Hillary Clinton but Not Donald Trump." *MarketWatch*. N.p., 07 Sept. 2016. Web. 2 Apr. 2017. <http://www.marketwatch.com/story/goldman-sachs-bans-top-staff-from-donating-to-trump-reports-2016-09-07-91031857>.

ISIS

1. "Cal Sarwar." *Goodreads*. N.p., n.d. Web. 4 Apr. 2017. <https://www.goodreads.com/author/show/8616688.Cal_Sarwar>.

2. "Newt Gingrich Quotes." *BrainyQuote*. Xplore, n.d. Web. 4 Apr. 2017. <https://www.brainyquote.com/quotes/quotes/n/newtgingri412534.html>.

3. "Sam Harris Quotes." *BrainyQuote*. Xplore, n.d. Web. 27 Mar. 2017. <https://www.brainyquote.com/quotes/quotes/s/samharris527730.html>.

4. Edmunds, Donna Rachel. "Steve Bannon Warned Us Islamic Terror Would Grip the West."*Breitbart*. N.p., 16 Nov. 2016. Web. 22 Apr. 2017. <http://www.breitbart.com/london/2016/11/16/steve-bannon-warned-us-islamic-terror-would-grip-the-west/>.

5. Lt. Col. Zumwalt, James. "The Islamic Ambush Awaiting Us." *WND*. N.p., 3 Mar. 2017. Web. 22 Apr. 2017. <http://www.wnd.com/2017/03/the-islamic-ambush-awaiting-us/>.

6. Kant, Garth. "Sebastian Gorka's Plan to Defeat ISIS – Simple but Devastating." *WND*. N.p., 26 June 2016. Web. 3 May 2017. <http://www.wnd.com/2016/06/sebastian-gorkas-plan-to-defeat-isis-simple-but-devastating/>.

7. Prestigiacomo, Amanda. "'Violent Torture Tools' Found in ISIS Prison For Female Sex Slaves [Video]." *Daily Wire*. N.p., 02 Sept. 2016. Web. 18 Apr. 2017. <http://www.dailywire.com/news/8865/violent-torture-tools-found-isis-prisons-female-amanda-prestigiacomo#>.

8. Pleitgen, Frederik, Angela Dewan, James Griffiths, and Catherine E. Shoichet. "Berlin Attack: ISIS Claims It Inspired Truck Assault." *CNN*. Cable News Network, 20 Dec. 2016. Web. 8 Apr. 2017. <http://www.cnn.com/2016/12/20/europe/berlin-christmas-market-truck/index.html>.

9. Faiola, Anthony, Souad Mekhennet, and Stephanie Kirchner. "Berlin on High Alert as Search for Christmas Market Attacker Resumes." *The Washington Post*. WP Company, 20 Dec. 2016. Web. 2 May 2017. <https://www.washingtonpost.com/world/truck-rams-into-berlin-christmas-market-in-deliberate-attack-killing-12/2016/12/20/2c73c5ec-c63b-11e6-acda-59924caa2450_story.html?utm_term=.178240de92e8>.

10. "TERROR WARNING: ISIS Plots Brutal 2017 SLAUGHTER across Europe to Spark Apocalypse." *Express.co.uk*. Express.co.uk, 02 Dec. 2016. Web. 9 Apr. 2017. <http://www.express.co.uk/news/world/739078/Europol-terror-threat-Isis-germany-uk-belgium>.

11. History.com Staff. "Crusades." *History.com*. A&E Television Networks, 2010. Web. 20 Jan. 2017. <http://www.history.com/topics/crusades>.

12. Standwithus.com. "Muslim Brotherhood Fact Sheet." *Www. standwithus.com*. N.p., n.d. Web. 3 May 2017. <http://www.standwithus.com/news/article.asp?id=1757>.

13. Zumwalt, James. "Zumwalt: Fifteen Years After 9/11, What Have We Learned?" *Breitbart*. N.p., 11 Sept. 2016. Web. 19 Apr. 2017. <http://www.breitbart.com/national-security/2016/09/11/fifteen-years-911-learned/>.

14. Gabbard, Tulsi. "H.R.608 - 115th Congress (2017-2018): Stop Arming Terrorists Act."*Congress.gov*. N.p., 23 Jan. 2017. Web. 20 Apr. 2017. <https://www.congress.gov/bill/115th-congress/house-bill/608>.

15. Bremmer, Paul. "GLOBALISM AND ISLAM: AN 'UNHOLY ALLIANCE'." WORLDNETDAILY.COM, 21 Dec. 2016. Web. 2 Mar. 2017. <http://www.wnd.com/2016/12/globalism-and-islam-an-unholy-alliance/>.

Obama's Legacy

1. Smith, Ben. "Obama on Small-town Pa.: Clinging to Religion, Guns, Xenophobia."*POLITICO.* N.p., 11 Apr. 2008. Web. 13 May 2017. <http://www.politico.com/blogs/ben-smith/2008/04/obama-on-small-town-pa-clinging-to-religion-guns-xenophobia-007737>.

2. Norris, Chuck. "THE OBAMA-CLINTON CLOWARD-PIVEN LEGACY." WORLDNETDAILY.COM, 19 July 2015. Web. 4 Apr. 2017. <http://www.wnd.com/2015/07/the-obama-clinton-cloward-piven-legacy/>.

3. Huston, Warner Todd. "Obama Invites Rapper to White House, Despite Indictment for Violence." *Breitbart.* N.p., 19 Apr. 2016. Web. 20 May 2017. <http://www.breitbart.com/big-government/2016/04/19/obama-invites-indicted-rapper-white-house-youth-empowerment-program/>.

4. Bandler, Aaron. "7 Facts That Show Obama's Economic Recovery Has Been AWFUL." *Daily Wire.* N.p., 01 Aug. 2016. Web. 1 Apr. 2017. <http://www.dailywire.com/news/7970/7-facts-show-obamas-economic-recovery-has-been-aaron-bandler>.

5. Martel, Frances. "Fact-Check: Yes, Hillary Clinton and Barack Obama Have Refused to Say 'Radical Islamic Terrorism'."

Breitbart. N.p., 9 Oct. 2016. Web. 11 Mar. 2017. <http://www.breitbart.com/live/second-presidential-debate-fact-check-livewire/fact-check-yes-hillary-clinton-barack-obama-refused-say-radical-islamic-terrorism/>.

6. "Obama: 'If You like Your Health Care Plan, You'll Be Able to Keep Your Health Care Plan'."*Politifact.com*. N.p., n.d. Web. 12 Apr. 2017. <http://www.politifact.com/obama-like-health-care-keep/>.

7. Bandes, Jillian. "No Family Making Less than $250,000 a Year Will See Any Form of Tax Increase." *Townhall*. Townhall.com, 16 Dec. 2009. Web. 18 Apr. 2017. <https://townhall.com/tipsheet/jillianbandes/2009/12/16/no-family-making-less-than-$250,000-a-year-will-see-any-form-of-tax-increase-n670313>.

8. "A Re-hash of Obamacare Lies: Let's Make This Obamacare's Last Birthday." *Americans for Prosperity*. Americans for Prosperity, 23 Mar. 2016. Web. 15 Apr. 2017. <https://americansforprosperity.org/re-obamacare-lies-lets-make-obamacares-last-birthday/>.

9. Furchtgott-Roth, Diana. "7 Obamacare Failures That Have Hurt Americans." *MarketWatch*. N.p., 25 Mar. 2016. Web. 11 Apr. 2017. <http://www.marketwatch.com/story/7-obamacare-failures-that-have-hurt-americans-2016-03-24>.

10. DelReal, Jose A. "Obamacare Consultant under Fire for 'stupidity of the American Voter' Comment." *The Washington Post*. WP Company, 11 Nov. 2014. Web. 14 Apr. 2017. <https://www.washingtonpost.com/news/post-politics/wp/2014/11/11/obamacare-consultant-under-fire-for-stupidity-of-the-american-voter-comment/?utm_term=.188c785d7240>.

11. "Lynch Says Tarmac Meeting with Bill Clinton Was 'regrettable'." *Fox News.* FOX News Network, 19 Dec. 2016. Web. 14 Apr. 2017. <http://www.foxnews.com/politics/2016/12/19/lynch-says-tarmac-meeting-with-bill-clinton-was-regrettable.html>.

12. Watkins, Eli. "Bill Clinton Meeting Causes Headaches for Hillary." *CNN.* Cable News Network, 30 June 2016. Web. 11 Apr. 2017. <http://www.cnn.com/2016/06/29/politics/bill-clinton-loretta-lynch/index.html>.

13. Tuttle, Ian. "El Chapo's Capture Puts 'Operation Fast and Furious' Back in the Headlines."*National Review.* N.p., 21 Jan. 2016. Web. 25 Mar. 2017. <http://www.nationalreview.com/article/430153/fast-furious-obamas-first-scandal>.

14. Greenberg, Jon. "CNN's Tapper: Obama Has Used Espionage Act More than All Previous Administrations." *Politifact.com.* N.p., 10 Jan. 2014. Web. 12 May 2017. <http://www.politifact.com/punditfact/statements/2014/jan/10/jake-tapper/cnns-tapper-obama-has-used-espionage-act-more-all-/>.

15. "Bio: Thomas Drake." *Whistleblower.org.* N.p., n.d. Web. 7 Apr. 2017. <https://www.whistleblower.org/bio-thomas-drake>.

16. Vamburkar, Meenal. "Judge Napolitano, Fox Host Rip DOJ Targeting Fox Reporter: 'Don't Know How Jay Carney Sleeps At Night'." *Mediaite.* Mediaite, 21 May 2013. Web. 9 Apr. 2017. <http://www.mediaite.com/tv/judge-napolitano-fox-host-rip-doj-targeting-fox-reporter-dont-know-how-jay-carney-sleeps-at-night/>.

17. Corsi, Jerome. "NSA Documents Prove Surveillance of Donald Trump & His Family."*Infowars.* N.p., 20 Mar. 2017. Web. 11 May 2017. <https://www.infowars.com/nsa-documents-prove-surveillance-on-donald-trump-and-alex-jones/>.

18. Wisner, Matthew. "Mnuchin on Fannie And Freddie Funds Used to Pay for ObamaCare: It's True." *Fox Business.* Fox Business, 01 May 2017. Web. 15 May 2017. <http://www.foxbusiness.com/politics/2017/05/01/mnuchin-on-fannie-and-freddie-funds-used-to-pay-for-obamacare-its-true.html>.

19. Nolan, Lucas. "Google Bans 200 Publishers Following 'Fake News' Policy Update." *Breitbart.* N.p., 26 Jan. 2017. Web. 15 Feb. 2017. <http://www.breitbart.com/tech/2017/01/26/google-bans-200-publishers-following-fake-news-policy-update/>.

20. Durden, Tyler. "11 Deeply Alarming Facts About America's Crumbling Infrastructure."*ZeroHedge.* N.p., 17 Feb. 2017. Web. 4 Mar. 2017. <http://www.zerohedge.com/news/2017-02-17/11-deeply-alarming-facts-about-americas-crumbling-infrastructure>.

21. Riddell, Kelly. "Benghazi Report Points out Obama, Clinton Lies." *The Washington Times.* The Washington Times, 28 June 2016. Web. 15 Apr. 2017. <http://www.washingtontimes.com/news/2016/jun/28/benghazi-report-points-out-obama-clinton-lies/>.

22. Boyer, Dave. "VA Still Plagued by Problems Two Years after Scandal." *The Washington Times.* The Washington Times, 03 Apr. 2016. Web. 5 Apr. 2017. <http://www.washingtontimes.

com/news/2016/apr/3/va-still-plagued-by-problems-two-years-after-scand/>.

America's Way Forward

1. PJ Video. "Trump: 'There Is No Such Thing as a Global Anthem, a Global Currency, or a Global Flag'." *Video.* PJ Media, 24 Feb. 2017. Web. 7 May 2017. <https://pjmedia.com/video/trump-there-is-no-such-thing-as-a-global-anthem-a-global-currency-or-a-global-flag/>.

2. Biography.com Editors. "Gail Devers." *Biography.com.* A&E Networks Television, 05 Feb. 2016. Web. 25 Apr. 2017. <https://www.biography.com/people/gail-devers-40831>.

3. "Gail Devers Quotes." *BrainyQuote.* Xplore, n.d. Web. 17 May 2017. <https://www.brainyquote.com/quotes/quotes/g/gaildevers144884.html>.

4. "Donald Trump's Congress Speech (full Text)." *CNN.* Cable News Network, 01 Mar. 2017. Web. 25 Apr. 2017. <http://www.cnn.com/2017/02/28/politics/donald-trump-speech-transcript-full-text/index.html>.